COVENTRY CITY FC
A HISTORY IN 50 MATCHES

JONATHAN STRANGE

The History Press

To the memory of my Father

Frontispiece: Lady Godiva, Broadgate, Coventry.

First published 2004 by Tempus Publishing

Reprinted 2016 by
The History Press
The Mill, Brimscombe Port,
Stroud, Gloucestershire, GL5 2QG
www.tempus-publishing.com

British Library Cataloguing in Publication Data.
A catalogue record for this book is available from the British Library.

ISBN 978 0 7524 2718 0

Typesetting and origination by Tempus Publishing Limited
Printed and bound in Great Britain

Acknowledgements

`I am especially grateful to Jim Brown for providing me with so many of the photographs in this book and for his help in answering my queries.

I wish to thank Coventry City Football Club, News International and the Press Association for permission to make use of certain photographs, and David Brassington, Chris Lambert and Richard Woodfield for the use of others.

I am grateful to the *Evening Standard* for permission to include the cartoon by Hector Breeze.

I am also indebted in various ways to the following: David Brassington, Don Chalk, Rod Dean, Mark Denman, Rick Gekoski, Mark Georgevic, Ernie Hunt, Monica Stephenson, Ena Strange, and, in particular, Eric A. Thorn.

The wonderful British Library Newspaper Library has been an important source of information.

I have quoted from *Life and Labour in a 20th century city: The experience of Coventry*, edited by Bill Lancaster and Tony Mason.

I would like to acknowledge the following works: *Singer's to Sky Blues* by David Brassington, Rod Dean and Don Chalk, *Coventry City, A Complete Record 1883-1991*, compiled by Rod Dean, with David Brassington, Jim Brown and Don Chalk, *Coventry City Footballers, The Complete Who's Who 1908-1993,* by Martin and Paul O'Connor, *Coventry City, The Elite Era, A Complete Record* by Jim Brown.

Introduction

This book is a testament to the disproportionately large amount of my life I have devoted to following my favourite football club. How grateful I am that the club has been Coventry City and, consequently, for all the people I have met and for all the friendships I have made, particularly in Coventry City London Supporters' Club.

The story of Coventry City is not one of unremitting or illusory success – not just about a great Cup Final or outstanding games played during thirty-four years on football's front page. It is also about struggles and humiliations. The peaks and troughs are an allegory of life itself.

Out of an unusual childhood and uncertain youth, the club came to embrace a varied adulthood. It is the story of a city felled by the Blitz whose football team helped endorse its recovery in the 1960s, of the aspirations of barnstorming years in the 1930s, of that May day in 1987, but also of King's Lynn, Sutton and all those desperate final flings.

My choice of matches is the means to relating that story, fifty separate chapters centred around individual games. The pieces are complete in themselves but they also build into a continuous narrative, into which I have endeavoured to draw all the major events, personalities and other matches.

It is a story that will continue to grow – into old age and beyond.

Jonathan Strange
Wembley, 2004

50 Matches

18 April 1891	Singer's 1-0 Willenhall Pickwick	Birmingham and District Junior Cup Final
2 November 1901	Berwick Rangers 11-2 Coventry City	FA Cup Third Qualifying Round
3 March 1910	Coventry City 0-2 Everton	FA Cup Fourth Round
1 May 1920	Coventry City 2-1 Bury	Football League Division Two
28 April 1934	Coventry City 9-0 Bristol City	Football League Division Three (South)
2 May 1936	Coventry City 2-1 Torquay United	Football League Division Three (South)
4 February 1939	Newcastle United 0-4 Coventry City	Football League Division Two
19 April 1952	Coventry City 0-2 Sheffield Wednesday	Football League Division Two
8 January 1955	Huddersfield Town 3-3 Coventry City	FA Cup Third Round
25 November 1961	Coventry City 1-2 King's Lynn	FA Cup Second Round
25 March 1963	Coventry City 2-1 Sunderland	FA Cup Fifth Round
25 April 1964	Coventry City 1-0 Colchester United	Football League Division Three
13 April 1965	Coventry City 1-0 Queens Park Rangers	Football Combination Division Two
29 April 1967	Coventry City 3-1 Wolverhampton Wanderers	Football League Division Two
11 May 1968	Southampton 0-0 Coventry City	Football League Division One
15 April 1969	Wolverhampton Wanderers 1-1 Coventry City	Football League Division One
10 January 1970	Coventry City 3-0 Manchester City	Football League Division One
3 October 1970	Coventry City 3-1 Everton	Football League Division One
20 October 1970	Bayern München 6-1 Coventry City	European Fairs Cup Second Round First Leg
4 November 1972	Arsenal 0-2 Coventry City	Football League Division One
19 October 1974	Middlesbrough 4-4 Coventry City	Football League Division One
19 May 1977	Coventry City 2-2 Bristol City	Football League Division One
27 December 1977	Coventry City 5-4 Norwich City	Football League Division One
6 September 1980	Coventry City 3-1 Crystal Palace	Football League Division One
27 January 1981	Coventry City 3-2 West Ham United	Football League Cup Semi-Final First Leg

Coventry City, 5 January 1907. From left to right, back row: Beaman, J., Jones, H., Edwards, F.J., H.A. Whitehouse, Gilbert, H., Smith, E., Parks, W. Front row: Such, E., Arnold, T., Kinsey, L., A. Wright, Tooth, J.G.

4 May 1982	Southampton 5-5 Coventry City	Football League Division One
10 December 1983	Coventry City 4-0 Liverpool	Football League Division One
12 May 1984	Coventry City 2-1 Norwich City	Football League Division One
26 May 1985	Coventry City 4-1 Everton	Football League Division One
3 May 1986	Coventry City 2-1 Queens Park Rangers	Football League Division One
25 October 1986	Sheffield Wednesday 2-2 Coventry City	Football League Division One
14 March 1987	Sheffield Wednesday 1-3 Coventry City	FA Cup Sixth Round
12 April 1987	Coventry City 3-2 Leeds United	FA Cup Semi-Final
13 May 1987	Coventry City 1-0 Charlton Athletic	FA Youth Cup Final Second Leg
16 May 1987	Coventry City 3-2 Tottenham Hotspur	FA Cup Final
2 March 1988	Reading 1-1 Coventry City	Simod Cup Semi-Final
7 January 1989	Sutton United 2-1 Coventry City	FA Cup Third Round
11 February 1990	Nottingham Forest 2-1 Coventry City	Littlewoods Cup Semi-Final First Leg
28 November 1990	Coventry City 5-4 Nottingham Forest	Rumbelows League Cup Fourth Round
2 May 1992	Aston Villa 2-0 Coventry City	Barclays League Division One
19 December 1992	Coventry City 5-1 Liverpool	FA Premier League
9 May 1995	Tottenham Hotspur 1-3 Coventry City	FA Carling Premiership
8 April 1996	Manchester United 1-0 Coventry City	FA Carling Premiership
5 May 1996	Coventry City 0-0 Leeds United	FA Carling Premiership
11 May 1997	Tottenham Hotspur 1-2 Coventry City	FA Carling Premiership
3 January 1998	Liverpool 1-3 Coventry City	FA Cup Third Round
27 February 1999	Aston Villa 1-4 Coventry City	FA Carling Premiership
26 December 1999	Coventry City 3-2 Arsenal	FA Carling Premiership
5 May 2001	Aston Villa 3-2 Coventry City	FA Carling Premiership
25 January 2003	Rochdale 2-0 Coventry City	FA Cup Fourth Round

NB League tables show the standings at the beginning of a match

Right: Leslie Jones.

Far right: Bobby Davidson.

SINGER'S v. WILLENHALL PICKWICK

18 April 1891
Perry Barr
Birmingham and District Junior Cup Final
Singer's 1 Willenhall Pickwick 0

Coventry City started out by bicycle. During its journey, the club has witnessed many changes in society, not all of which have been for the better. Nowadays we turn a blind eye to cyclists who endanger pedestrians by riding their bikes on street pavements.

In 1883, Dr William Price of Llantrisant provoked legal action in his pursuit of a more unusual expedient. To general outrage, he cremated the remains of his son in full public view. In February of the following year the judge presiding over the case ruled that cremation was legal, provided that no nuisance was caused to others. Had the ruling come a few months earlier, Karl Marx could have spared pilgrims the subsequent trudge up Highgate Hill by submitting his own remains to this alternative procedure.

1883 was the year when the bacteriologist Robert Koch described a preventive inoculation against anthrax; Mussolini was born, Wagner died; a ten-storey skyscraper rose above Chicago and, for the first time, the Orient Express rumbled across Europe.

Today, fifty-eight years after the defeat of Hitler, the British remain suspicious of a European commitment. In 1883, sixty-eight years after the defeat of Napoleon, Britain was less coy at engaging with others.

It was the British who spread the gospel of games, and well beyond the heart of the Empire. USA v. Canada is an even older cricket fixture than England v. Australia. What we now call AC Milan was founded by an Englishman, Alfred Edwards, as the Milan Cricket and Football Club. To this day, Italians correctly refer to the club as Milan, not Milano.

A few miles from Coventry, in the days before Tom Brown, the Rugby schoolboy, William Webb Ellis, picked up the ball and ran with it. Rugger established more of a hold in the Coventry area than soccer, but it is soccer which remains the most widespread sporting legacy of the British.

At the end of the nineteenth century, Coventry was a city of great economic and social change. The decline of the traditional crafts of ribbon-weaving and watchmaking precipitated a search for

Singer's 1885. From left to right, back row: H. Hathaway (captain), A. Poole, H. Barnacle, W. Hardy, J. Collins, Mr Smith. Middle row: T. Dowell, C. Heath. Front row: H. Banks, G. Bowers, J. Grady, F. Moseley, S. Turner.

A Singer's advertisement.

new sources of wealth and employment which, in the 1880s, was rewarded by the birth of the cycle trade. Coventry soon emerged as the principal centre of the cycle industry in Britain, attracting many of the leading inventors and entrepreneurs. In 1881, sixteen cycle manufacturers were resident in Coventry, and this figure rose to more than seventy during the boom years of the mid-1890s. The bicycle, economically, was the child of the sewing machine. George Singer had been an employee of the Coventry Sewing Machine Company. When Singer became Mayor of Coventry in 1891, he symbolised Coventry's transition from a craft-based society to one which was shortly to become fully integrated with modern industrial capitalism. Cycle manufacture turned to motor car manufacture. Eventually, in 1956, the ailing Singer company was taken over by Rootes, which in turn was later rescued by Chrysler.

In October 1883, a group of machinists from Singer's gathered at the Aylesford Inn in Hillfields. Under the leadership of William Stanley, Singer's Football Club was conceived. The club would one day become Coventry City. Singer's had their first pitch in Dowell's Field off the Binley Road and the landlord of the White Lion at Gosford Green made a changing room available to the team. The first match resulted in a 12-1 victory against the Royal Artillery. George Singer was club president, although his brother-in-law J.C. Stringer was more actively involved. In 1884, Singer's joined the Birmingham County FA but it was not until J.G. Morgan became secretary in 1887 that the club began to organise itself with real purpose. In that year, Singer's acquired a pitch close to Swan Lane, adjacent to where the modern stadium eventually stood, which became the Stoke Road ground. This was a genuine enclosure with a twopenny admission price. There was also a small grandstand. It was during this period that maximum pitch lengths were reduced from 200 to 150 yards and goal nets were introduced.

Under Morgan, a set of fixtures was prearranged and entry made into the Birmingham and District Junior Cup, in which Singer's first appeared in 1887 with a 4-0 win against Bournville Villa. The team reached the semi-finals and matches were beginning to attract several hundred spectators. By the time the AGM was held at the White Lion in 1888 the Singer's club had become fully constituted.

A further successful Birmingham Cup run prompted these comments from a columnist in the *Coventry Mercury*:

> I am firmly of the opinion that the association game is destined ere long to exceed in the public estimation the time-honoured rugby rules in Coventry. Up to the present the pick-up game has held full sway in the city, from the fact that the dribbling code – what there has been of it – found no favour with us. Now however, a change is gradually being brought about and a game that only one or two seasons ago was looked upon with indifference in Coventry is rapidly gaining in public favour.

Two thousand people turned out in dense fog at Stoke Road to watch new opponents Aston Villa Reserves, but it was the local rivalry with Rudge that was to prove intense. The practise of employers sponsoring their workers' leisure stems from far back in the nineteenth century. J.J. Cash, ribbon weavers, had established a cricket club before the 1880s. Cash's were Quakers but Alfred Herbert too was later to encourage his employees to play team games as part of the family firm paternalism which he sought to foster. Rudge-Whitworth had already formed a cycle club for employees and were to promote an annual sports day, open to all-comers.

Singer's and Rudge were involved in litigation on various occasions. Competitiveness also extended to the football field and was sometimes bitter. A month before beating Rudge 5-0 at the Butts Stadium, five Singer's players were assisting police with their enquiries after a skirmish with Rudge supporters at the Trafalgar Arms. Charges against one of them, Teddy Kirk, 'for stabbing a Rudge supporter in the buttocks with a dagger', were dismissed. Kirk was carried shoulder-high from the court by his supporters. The popular goalkeeper was one of the outstanding players of the early years. In those days, the laws of the game afforded goalkeepers little protection. 'Little Teddy' accepted this with equanimity, but on one occasion he took exception and rendered an uppercut to a Small Heath forward which laid his opponent out cold.

Football excursions were not a Coventry City invention of the 1960s. In February 1890, a special train carrying 800 supporters steamed out of Coventry station on its way to a cup game at Small Heath. The game resulted in a 'near-fatal' injury to the captain, Joe Collins, but the club again reached the semi-finals of the Birmingham Cup.

By the beginning of the 1890/91 season, Collins had been replaced and Joe Briggs had left to become a Benedictine monk. Tom Bird had taken over as captain and there was a new centre forward, Frank Mobley. Mobley was a prolific goalscorer who went on to play First Division football for Bury.

Singer's were a small team and their size, along with their black and red shirts, earned them the nickname 'Little Blackbirds'. This time, Singer's went one better in the Birmingham Cup when they beat Packington 5-0 in the semi-finals. The final was held at Aston Villa's Perry Barr ground and 2,500 made the journey from Coventry, 1,000 of them on special trains and most of the rest on bicycles. There was a crowd of almost 6,000. The phenomenon of large numbers of people gathering to watch sporting events such as football had taken root within a fairly short space of time.

Singer's, Birmingham and District Junior Cup Winners, 1891. From left to right, top row: J.G. Morgan (Hon. Sec), T. Cashmore, W. Hughes, W. Glew, E. Kirk, W. Edmunds, W. Howell, T. Cannings, F. Moseley, (Umpire). From left to right, bottom row: H. Banks, C. Pretty, F. Mobley, T. Bird, Capt, W. Dorrell.

The start of the match was delayed when a strange situation with referee I. Hassey prompted a change of official. The *Mercury* reported:

> Midway through the first half, Singer's launched the crucial attack. The ball was kept bobbing around near the Pickwicks' goal. Then Harry Banks found Frank Mobley, and with a fair daisy-cutter he beat the Pickwick 'keeper and Singer's had scored the first goal amid a scene which baffles description.

It was Banks' last competitive match. Consumption, that rampant killer, was to claim 'Little Harry' less than four years later.

The celebrations in Coventry were tumultuous. Telegrams quickly spread the news. Most of the population of the old town were in the streets to welcome home the team. The *Mercury* wrote:

> Singer's' own Apollo band was there to lead them aloft a horse-drawn carriage on a triumphal procession into Broadgate. Also there to greet them were their local rivals the Rudge, carrying a banner saying: 'Hearty congratulations from the Rudge to Singer's.' Their triumphal path was lit by a series of coloured fires and when the coach reached the narrow Hertford Street, the crowd was so dense that it brought the procession to a halt. Women screamed and children cried to be delivered from the horse hooves and coach wheels.

When they arrived at the Queen's Hotel, George Singer was waiting with a well-earned banquet. Outside, the band played on and the throng sang 'Auld Acquaintance' and 'Good Old Singer's Never Rust'.

In the same year, Coventry Rugby Club won the Midland Counties Cup and its junior version too. 'The city of three spires is now the city of three cups', said the *Mercury*. The local tobacco importer David Cooke was inspired by events. He commemorated the achievement by introducing his 'Three Cups Tobacco'. Cooke was later to become the greatest benefactor in the history of Coventry City.

Berwick Rangers v. Coventry City

2 November 1901
Severn Terrace
FA Cup Third Qualifying Round
Berwick Rangers 11 Coventry City 2

In 1967, Berwick Rangers knocked Glasgow Rangers out of the Scottish Cup. It is probably the most sensational result in the history of Scottish football. However, the club that beat Coventry City in 1901 was a long way from the salmon shoals of the river Tweed. These Berwick Rangers came from Worcester. The club was a precursor of Worcester City.

The Berwick Rangers ground happened to be next to the racecourse. At the start of the Edwardian age, horse racing was rivalled only by the music hall in the extent of its public appeal.

Manchester United were not the first club to pull out of the FA Cup when it suited them. Coventry City withdrew from their tie at Oswestry in 1900 in order to play a Birmingham League game. A year later, Coventry were forced to fulfil their fixture against Ironbridge when the Birmingham League refused to sanction a postponement but this time they decided not to scratch from the Cup. City did not have a reserve team, so a side was hastily assembled from local league players to make the journey to Worcester whilst the regulars played out a goalless draw at Highfield Road. Apart from a 14-1 defeat away to Aston Villa Reserves in 1900, this remains City's heaviest defeat in a competitive 'first-team' match. Even one of City's goals was scored by an opponent. Berwick Rangers went on to lose 2-1 at Walsall in the next round.

Singer's first entered the FA Cup in 1892. On account of Burton Swifts' league commitments, the tie was played at eight o'clock on a Wednesday morning. In 1897, the team were on the wrong end of their first giant-killing when they lost to a village side called Wrockwardine Wood.

There were several important developments in the 1890s. In 1892, as well as retaining the Birmingham Junior Cup, Singer's won both the Walsall Cup and the Wednesbury Cup. The latter, after a lot of shenanigans, was shared. In the semi-finals, Singer's met the professionals of Wednesbury Old Athletic. With the scores level at 1-1, Wednesbury declined to play extra time. Singer's claimed victory, but a replay was ordered at Perry Barr. When their opponents failed to turn up, Singer's went through the formality of walking the ball over the goal line and again claimed the tie but the Wednesbury FA contrived to disqualify Singer's. Athletic went on to beat Hanley Town in the final but George Singer himself threatened legal action against the Wednesbury FA. The Football Association ordered the Birmingham FA to oversee the case. Clearly, Athletic had not wished to lose to a Junior club, and they were eventually forced to share the trophy with Singer's.

In the 1890s, the city of Coventry was becoming overcrowded and there was a chronic housing shortage. Police reported in 1896 that there had never been so many people walking the streets at night searching for a place to sleep. The cycle industry could be uncertain despite its size, and a bad slump had hit the Singer's works. Consequently, the football club lost four first-team players. A decision was taken to go professional, but in effect this resulted in just a handful of players receiving expenses and appearance money. It remained a works team represented only by those employed at the cycle works. In 1894, Singer's joined the Birmingham League. Despite two reasonable seasons between 1897 and 1899, results were poor and debts were beginning to mount. In 1895, new secretary Tom Cashmore set about reducing the debt by organising a concert at the Sydenham Palace Opera House. The young George Robey was among those on the bill.

In 1898, the Little Blackbirds' feathers turned blue and white as Singer's became Coventry City. There was an objection from Coventry Rugby Club over a possible confusion of names. Some years later, on their way home from a fixture in London, the City team were approached by the station-master at Euston. 'Are you the Coventry football team?', he asked. After confirming their identity, the City players and officials were shown into the station restaurant, wined and dined, and put on the train home to Coventry. Not long after, a ravenous Coventry Rugby Club arrived, too late for dinner.

In April 1899, the City players were asked to give up their salaries for the rest of the season to enable the club to meet its debts. The players went on strike and only three of the regular first team took part in the final game at Hereford.

The Stoke Road ground was to be taken over for building development. The football club acquired a 6½ acre site from the Craven Cricket Club and the football ground we have come to know began to take shape. A 2,000-seater grandstand was erected, which remained until 1936. Coventry City kicked off at Highfield Road for the first time on 9 September 1899 with a 1-0 win against Shrewsbury Town. There was a crowd of 3,000.

Some appalling results were to follow. After a friendly against Hinckley, the *Coventry Mercury* reporter commented:

> A more miserable exhibition of football I have never witnessed. Some of the City players came onto the field in a deplorable condition – I might use a much stronger term – they brought disgrace on themselves and the club. Surely something can be done by the executive to stop this kind of unseemly conduct, with paid players too.

A month into the 1900/01 season, there was a dispute between the players and the committee over unfulfilled contracts. The club received a two-match ban and a fine from the FA, as well as an order to satisfy the players' demands.

This was the winter when the river Sherbourne rose to unprecedented levels, causing the worst floods in the city's history. The football club announced that all receipts from the game against Brierley Hill Alliance would go to the Flood Relief Fund. Three days before the game came news of the death of Queen Victoria.

It was to be seventy years before the chief football reporter of the *Evening Telegraph* advertised his identity for the first time. Successive generations wrote under the byline of 'Nemo'. Having focussed on the Ironbridge match, Derek Henderson's predecessor summed up the Berwick game as follows:

> It was hardly expected that the City would win, but it was certainly not anticipated that the Rangers would win by the large majority of eleven goals to two. Dipple is a custodian whom one deemed capable of better things than letting the ball go past his charge on eleven occasions, seven in the first half and four in the second. It was certainly a gala day for the Rangers, who scored five goals in the first half-hour's play, and practically never gave the City a look in – they could score only once in each half. Comment on the match is superfluous. Eleven goals to two – truly it was a 'staggerer'.

COVENTRY CITY v. EVERTON

3 March 1910
Highfield Road
FA Cup Fouth Round
Coventry City 0 Everton 2

The Edwardian era had nine weeks left to run. Professional football was well established. Less than twenty years before, Singer's had been sparring with Rudge, their rivals on the cycle assembly line, for supremacy within Coventry itself. Entry to the Birmingham League in 1894 brought the team into competition with the reserve sides of Aston Villa, Birmingham, Burslem Port Vale, Stoke, West Bromwich and Wolves, as well as the cream of other teams in the area.

One day, the great Wilf Mannion would play for King's Lynn, Coventry's Dietmar Bruck for Weymouth. The Southern League, during the decades before Beazer Homes and the 'Pyramid', was a pasture for ex-League players to stroll among the daisies before being sent to the knackers. However, at the time when the Chief Constable of Coventry extolled the virtues of Coventry City's application, the Southern League was much more than that. It was a rival to the Football League with attendances slightly higher than those in the Second Division. The spine was made up of clubs who were later to join the Third Division on its establishment in the early 1920s. The fixture list looked like a run round of the sides the Sky Blues were to escaped from with Jimmy Hill.

In 1905 Coventry were taken over by a syndicate headed by Fred Lee. Lee was instrumental in bringing about another important development. Prompted by complaints from the old committee, an FA Commission held an inquiry into the club. The upshot was that in 1907 Coventry City became a private limited company.

The colourfulness of Coventry matches of the early 1900s lies less in the quality of the performances than in the events surrounding them. In one fractious game at West Bromwich, three second-half penalties were given against City. Following the award of one of them, the City players prevented the kick from being taken by repeatedly kicking the ball off the spot and then hoofing it into the crowd. When the West Brom player was eventually allowed to proceed, he missed. There was an inquiry and Coventry were heavily fined. Two weeks later, the boot was on the other foot when 'City players were treated to much bustling, kicking and general abuse before escaping down the street back to the safety of the changing rooms pursued by the howling mob'. Halesowen's unbeaten home record had been brought to an end.

In 1907/08, Coventry enjoyed a nine-match FA Cup run – including a replayed tie at Bilston after the first game had been abandoned due to a 'tornado'. Having played through the qualifiers, City lost to Crystal Palace in the first round. A gate of nearly 10,000 made such an impression on Palace officials that they were to speak up strongly on behalf of Coventry's application to join the Southern League. In the week prior to the game, the City players had relaxed at Droitwich by taking brine baths. The stars of the side were Albert Lewis and John Tooth, local man Fred Chaplin and the forwards 'Tubby' Warren and Billy Smith. The 43 goal tally of the teenaged Smith was only ever exceeded by Clarrie Bourton. In April, City played five league games in six days to catch up with their programme. They finished this, their last and most successful season in the Birmingham League, in fourth place and signed off with a record 11-2 win against West Brom.

Bradford Park Avenue, who had somewhat bizarrely spent the only year of their existence in the Southern League, joined the Football League along with Tottenham. Coventry, Exeter and Southend were elected to the Southern League. City's first game was against Crystal Palace. The local reporter

GALLAHER'S CIGARETTES.

C. TICKLE,
COVENTRY CITY, 1909-10.

Right: Bob Evans.

Far right: Charlie
Tickle.

wrote: 'Within an hour of the advertised time of the kick-off there was a decided improvement as though Jupiter Pluvius, knowing the monetary need of the City Executive, had for pity's sake restrained his mighty aqueous forces in order to concentrate on some less memorable day.'

During the same year, the lightweight-looking Coventry team acquired a new nickname: 'The Bantams'. At the end of their first season in the Southern League, the Bantams finished second from bottom, but there were some talented newcomers to the side, such as the two wingers, Charlie Tickle and Harry Buckle. David Cooke, whose Three Cups tobacco had celebrated the Birmingham Cup win of 1891, joined the board in 1909. Buckle became player/manager and Cooke's money enabled him to buy goalkeeper Bob Evans, who was to become the first Coventry player to win an international cap, and Eli Bradley, the frustrated West Brom penalty-taker of a few years before.

The circumstances of Bradley's marriage are worthy of note. After failing to get parental consent, he and his girlfriend had to meet clandestinely, and a secret marriage was planned in May 1908. However, the future bride's parents got wind of the affair and the girl was snatched from the arms of her lover at the Registry Office. Her tears and protestations were too much for her parents, and they were forced to release her. The ceremony took place several hours later.

Evans and Bradley were followed by a forward by the name of Elias Henry O'Hanrahan, probably the most famous person ever to play for Coventry City. Despite playing for England in a Victory International in 1919 and giving stout service to Brentford in the early 1920s, it is as one of England's very greatest batsmen that he is celebrated. O'Hanrahan was none other than 'Patsy' Hendren. Hendren joined Middlesex towards the end of cricket's Golden Age, established himself as the finest middle-order batsman of the 1920s and won 51 caps. Only Jack Hobbs and Frank Woolley ever exceeded his 57,611 runs in first-class cricket and only Hobbs has his 170 centuries. In 1920, *Wisden* also described him as 'about the finest outfield in the kingdom'. R.C. Robertson-Glasgow captured the essence of the universal love for the man:

I think that he most enjoyed doing something outrageous when the scene was all majesty and strain. Perhaps it was the crisis of some Test match. He saw the serious doctors bending anxiously over the patient. He saw rows of faces in the crowd like flock upon flock of sheep, absorbing the wonted pabulum, relieved by some

15

incredible ass in a horned handkerchief, who was plainly doomed to bore whole families for whole weeks with bleating stories of the wonderful play. He saw the pavilion members, righteously conscious of privileged accommodation, some affecting knowledge, others sobriety; next to them, the gentlemen of the Press, poising the knowing pencil, forging a paragraph from a no-ball, making a sermon of a cut. And his demon whispered to him: 'Hendren, for heaven's sake do something funny.' And he'd do it.

Coventry City soon found their feet in the Southern League but it was the FA Cup performances that drew attention. In 1909/10, qualifying-round wins against Wrexham and Kettering earned City a first-round tie at Preston. Preston may no longer have been invincible but they were still a powerful First Division side. A goal down for most of the game, the Bantams fought back to win 2-1. A 1-0 victory at Southern League rivals Portsmouth in the second round was followed by a 3-1 home win over First Division Nottingham Forest. City were into the quarter-finals and paired with another First Division side, Everton.

Coventry turned down Everton's invitation to switch the tie to Goodison Park and laid hands on every available piece of furniture to accommodate the record crowd of 19,095. Match receipts of £1,000 substantially paid for a new stand, which was only replaced in 1964 when the Sky Blue Stand was built. The game itself was a disappointment, although Hendren probably enjoyed some banter with Everton's England international left-half and Lancashire cricketer, Henry Makepeace. Hendren and Makepeace were to bat together for England in the Ashes series in Australia in 1920/21. The Toffees ran out 2-0 winners, both goals being scored by England centre forward Bertie Freeman. Everton then lost their semi-final against Barnsley.

Coventry took another First Division scalp, Sheffield Wednesday, in 1910/11. There were 2,000 City supporters who made the trip to Hillsborough, or Owlerton as it was still called. Billy Meredith was in the Manchester United team that won 5-1 on its first visit to Highfield Road in the second round in February 1912.

In October 1910, the club got into trouble when, as a result of deciding to save money by travelling on a later train, the team arrived grotesquely late for a Southern League fixture at Northampton. The train had broken down at Long Buckby and the game, scheduled for 3.30, kicked-off at 4.58, with most of the Coventry team still pulling on their shorts. Inevitably, the game was eventually abandoned because of bad light. The ref had no doubt proceeded in the fear that some hitherto patient customers might become restive without a token gesture of entertainment. The Cobblers' manager was Herbert Chapman. He had clearly already grasped the diplomatic demands of great management when he wrote in the *Northampton Daily Echo*: 'I feel assured, however, no one regrets the inconvenience and annoyance our supporters were subjected to more than the Coventry executive...'

A useful side began to take shape, with the likes of full-back Dick Barnacle. Brentford were slaughtered 9-0 at Christmas 1911 and the Bantams went on to finish sixth. However, after another Cup defeat by Manchester United in 1912/13, form fell away. It collapsed completely a year later with City finishing bottom of the table. At this point the team also lost its highly respected trainer, Eleander Juggins. Relegation brought an almost exclusively Welsh fixture list at the beginning of the Great War. Trips to the likes of Mid Rhondda, Pontypridd and Ton Pentre were costly. Only three of the other twelve clubs – Brentford, Stalybridge Celtic and Stoke City – were from outside Wales. The Southern League did offer subsidies to the English travellers, but they were minimal. Seven weeks after beating Newport 10-1, City lost 9-1 at Stoke. Gates were down, the financial situation was deteriorating and the club was even summonsed for non-payment of rates. When Frank Scott-

Above: Highfield Road 1910.

Right: 'Patsy' Hendren, Middlesex and England.

Walford departed after a brief spell as manager to take up a government appointment, he was owed £100 in unpaid wages.

The club decided to leave the Southern League. They applied to join the Central League but received only two votes. On suspension of organised football in 1915, Coventry City were in a desperate situation and an altogether parlous state.

Coventry had been the first club to reduce their wages in the 1914/15 season but this was probably less out of respect for the national situation than for reasons of financial expediency. Despite the 'Home by Christmas' optimism, there was widespread criticism that football – unlike rugby – was not immediately abandoned in 1914. But it was probably more than distaste that moved the *Coventry Herald* to comment: 'When the war is over and football resumes, one certainly expects to see Coventry Rugby Club once again the most popular as in older days and Coventry a distinctly rugby town'. Coventry City were close to extinction.

17

COVENTRY CITY V. BURY

1 May 1920
Highfield Road
Football League Division Two
Coventry City 2 Bury 1

	P	W	D	L	F	A	W	D	L	F	A	GA	P
20 Coventry City	41	6	7	7	18	25	2	4	15	15	47	0.4583	27
21 Lincoln City	41	8	6	7	27	30	1	3	16	15	67	0.4330	27
22 Grimsby Town	41	7	4	9	20	23	2	1	18	11	51	0.4189	23

'Bungs' paid in motorway service areas and bent Oriental betting syndicates were not the beginning and end of bribery and corruption in British football. From Billy Meredith in 1905 to Tony Kay and Peter Swan in the 1960s and later Bruce Grobbelaar, many a name has been implicated. The events surrounding the Coventry/Bury game of 1920 are among the most disgraceful in the history of the Football League.

The coming of peace in 1918 coincided with a worldwide influenza epidemic that claimed twenty million lives. At the start of that same winter of 1918/19, Coventry City – who had been saved from extinction by David Cooke – joined an unofficial Midlands section of the Football League. They were able to field several outstanding guest players who had been drawn to Coventry by the munitions industry. The team impressed with the way they acquitted themselves and for the substantial support they attracted.

Official League football returned on 30 August 1919. There were forty-four clubs split into two divisions, compared with forty in 1915. Stoke City, once founder members, had already been elected in 1915 in place of Glossop, and Coventry City, Rotherham County, South Shields, and West Ham United were elected in 1919. After only eight games of the new League programme, Leeds City were expelled for 'irregular practices' and Port Vale took over their fixtures.

Coventry's early years in the Football League were a turbulent and unremitting struggle, both on and off the field. It all began with a 5-0 home defeat by Tottenham. It took ten games for City to get even a point, and only 4 goals were scored in the opening 19 fixtures. The first win did not come until Christmas Day. City had gone eleven matches without a goal (only Hartlepool United in 1993 have played more minutes without scoring) when they recorded that 3-2 victory against Stoke City.

Goalscoring became more of a habit under Harry Pollitt, who was appointed manager in November. By March, City were off the bottom of the table for the first time. However, the perception was that if Coventry finished in the bottom two they would not get re-elected. Since the Football League and the Southern League were at loggerheads, it was possible that City might even find themselves with nowhere to go. With two games remaining, both against Bury, City were a point behind Lincoln with a game in hand. Grimsby had lost touch at the bottom.

Many years later, club captain George Chaplin told the *Coventry Herald* what happened:

> With a couple of matches left things looked so bad that I had a talk with the chairman, David Cooke. We decided that something must be done. The outcome of it all was that I went to Bury with £200 in my pocket and when I left I had the feeling that City's prospects of gaining three points from the two games with Bury were not such a remote possibility.

Left: Harry Pollitt.

Centre: George Chaplin.

Right: David Cooke.

City drew 2-2 at Gigg Lane. A week later, in front of a record crowd at Highfield Road of 23,506, Bury were a goal up at half-time. Chaplin went on to describe how one of the Bury players came into the dressing room and told him that City were so poor that Bury could not lose, however badly they played. However, even without Alec Mercer's two second-half goals, City would have been safe. Lincoln lost at Huddersfield and were not subsequently re-elected. Grimsby became members of the newly formed Third Division. 'While the City supporters were celebrating the club's escape that night I kept an appointment in the cloakroom of the King's Head Hotel where I handed over the final instalment of the sum agreed without a word being spoken,' said Chaplin.

Form did not improve the following season. The Bantams slipped from twentieth to twenty-first and were bottom of the table for six months. They stayed up because only one side, Stockport County, were relegated. Twenty new clubs were admitted in 1921/22 with the Third Division, after its only season, split into North and South sections. Another dreadful season, with City finishing twentieth, did nothing to undermine the constancy of the Coventry public. Indeed, over the club's first three seasons, attendances averaged nearly 16,500. In 1919/20, only Tottenham, Birmingham and West Ham attracted a higher average in the Second Division, and City enjoyed better support throughout the first five seasons than at least ⅔ of their rivals. Even when the average dipped beneath 10,000 after relegation in 1925, only one team in the Third Division (North), Bradford Park Avenue, were better supported.

Rumours had been circulating about the Bury matches for some time, but it was not until 29 May 1923 that a commission appointed by the Football League issued the following terse statement: 'The Commission is satisfied that an arrangement was made between Bury and Coventry City allowing the latter to win'. Had the rumours surfaced earlier, when all the guilty parties were still involved with their clubs, Bury and Coventry would almost certainly have been thrown out of the League. David Cooke, who served Coventry as director, chairman and president, was suspended from football for life, along with fellow director Jack Marshall, and George Chaplin. Seven players and officials from Bury received life bans and the clubs were each fined £100. Two years later, Harry Pollitt, who was probably no longer working in football, was also banned.

Many felt that the club were fortunate to remain in the League. The *Birmingham Sports Argus* commented: 'They have proved a danger to the game which will be better for their ostracism'.

COVENTRY CITY v. BRISTOL CITY

28 April 1934
Highfield Road
Football League Division Three (South)
Coventry City 9 Bristol City 0

Coventry City's biggest Football League victory came at a bountiful time in the club's history. There was plenty of fun in the 1930s for those who flocked to Highfield Road. The public was transported by the bravado of its local team and the abundance of goals.

It took the Bantams a long time to find their feet. The 1920s had been as grim as the 1930s were optimistic. In 1927, the *Birmingham Sports Argus* wrote: 'Since their arrival in the Football League in 1919 Coventry City has always been a storm centre'. Hence, the 1920s became known as the 'Stormy Period'. In their first twelve years in the League there were five different boards of management and eight different people in charge of the team. Coventry's best position in their first six seasons after being elected was fifth from bottom.

Shareholders successfully sought the resignation of the board in 1922 but the new chairman, W.J. Harris, lasted only a year. Relegation to the Third Division (North) in 1925 brought another vote of no confidence. City were transferred to the Third Division (South) the following season which meant that on eventual promotion to the First Division they became the only club ever to play in all six divisions of the Football League.

Coventry-born Albert Evans, a member of Aston Villa's double-winning side in 1896/97, succeeded Harry Pollitt as manager in 1920. Given the financial constraints, Evans did well to keep Coventry in the League but he 'resigned' in November 1924. After leaving football, he went on to pursue an adventurous life which included a spell of gold prospecting in the Yukon.

By March 1922, directors were trying to raise spirits by seeking a new image for the club. The blue and white shirts were replaced for a couple of seasons by green and red halves (Coventry's civic colours). However, a massive majority of supporters voted to retain the nickname of 'The Bantams' despite new suggestions such as 'The Velocipedes', 'The Oojahs' and 'The Scrapers'.

In November 1925, Coventry City's blossoming legacy of humiliation in the FA Cup was splendidly endorsed with defeat by Midland League Worksop, many of whose players had been on the morning shift down the pit. James Kerr was now the City manager. Some senior players were upset by the departure of Evans, and Kerr's recruitment of several anonymous newcomers from his native Scotland prompted the *Evening Telegraph* to comment: 'City fans have little desire to watch Coventry Celtic'. At the last home game of the season against Hartlepools, supporters organised a boycott resulting in the lowest ever League attendance at Highfield Road of 1,660.

By 1927, there were at least improvements to the ground with the club purchasing a stand from the RFU at Twickenham. However, by November, things had got so bad on the field that *Nemo* in the *Evening Telegraph* was moved to comment:

> The supporters' opinion of the club is that they are on a parallel with the mule, in so far as the club is without pride of ancestry or hope of posterity... The events of the past few seasons have been enough to draw tears from the rotting planks of the old main stand... I shall be fit for nothing but the writing of funeral dirges.

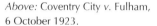

Top: Coventry City, 1923/24.

Jimmy Dougall and Danny Shea.

Above: Coventry City *v.* Fulham,
6 October 1923.

How often would supporters of Coventry and other teams come to invoke his opinion that 'We shall continue to struggle until money is spent on the purchase of first-class players'. Kerr was sacked in March 1928. He died from pneumonia six years later.

City went to Northampton for the last game of the 1927/28 season facing the prospect of re-election. With the events of 1920 still fresh in many minds, re-election might not have been forthcoming. A dubious Northampton goal sparked a riot among the Coventry followers and the referee was knocked unconscious by a stone at the end of the game. There were no transistors to enlighten oiks of Merthyr's defeat at Exeter.

A few weeks earlier, a cheque, for the purchase of Notts County's Norman Dinsdale and Alf Widdowson, had bounced. The club's saviour, yet again, was David Cooke. In 1910, Cooke had mainly been responsible for paying for the new stand. In 1917, with the club facing closure, he paid off three-and-a-half years' rent on Highfield Road and became the sole tenant of the ground, which he remained until his death in 1932. He paid all the costs of City joining the League and, in 1922, cancelled £15,400 owing to him. Up to this time, he was the sole guarantor of the club's debt with the bank. In 1928, he presented City with a Daimler, the club's first official car. The first season in the League resulted in a loss of £7,000, which went mainly on transfer fees, and was sustained by Cooke's generosity. Cooke said: 'What money I possess I have made in Coventry, and if I can do anything to further the interests of Coventry City I feel I should do it.' Cooke remained loyal to this despite the life ban incurred as a result of his part in the Bury scandal. At his death, he again wrote off the club's debts.

In 1928, the entire board was voted out and Walter Brandish became chairman. James McIntyre, the ex-City player and trainer, was enlisted as manager. He introduced 'McIntyre's Ticket', a set of rules which forbade, among other things, attendance at whist drives. Under McIntyre, results at last began to improve, despite a 10-2 thrashing at Norwich on 15 March 1930 – the club's heaviest League defeat. There was further boardroom rancour when Brandish desired to replace McIntyre. Brandish had his way. The 'stormy period' was coming to an end and the appointment of Harry Storer in April 1931 was the seminal moment.

Storer's family had made a name at both cricket and football. Storer was ten when his goalkeeper father died of tuberculosis. He won 2 England caps with Derby County and, after becoming Coventry manager, continued to open the batting for Derbyshire until the end of the 1936 season in which they won the County Championship for the only time. Another member of the Derbyshire XI was Charlie Elliott, who had been one of Storer's first signings for Coventry. Brian Clough, whose partner Peter Taylor was a protégé of Storer's second stint at Coventry, described him as a 'wiry little bugger, with a tough reputation'. Storer later told Clough: 'Look at your players prior to the coach leaving and count the hearts. If there are less than five, don't bother setting off.' Storer was an almost messianic advocate of discipline and it was around this that the successful Coventry teams of the 1930s were built. However, while there was a strong element of the sergeant-major about him, Storer respected genuine talent. The quality and ebullience of his Coventry teams stemmed from more than mere square-bashing.

The inadequacy of City's teams during their early League years would have unnerved many a loyal custodian as he stood behind them. Nevertheless, despite stretching to only 5ft 7in and having been shot in the arm during the war, Jerry Best became one of the giants of the side. George Chaplin was an outstanding right-back before his excommunication and 'Cute' Herbert scored over eighty goals. Right-winger Jimmy Dougall, full-back Jackie Randle and a portly former England international, Danny Shea, were among others of note. Jimmy Loughlin scored almost a goal a game in 1929/30 and 'Shadow' Allen proved a worthy successor to Best. 'Twinkletoes' Toseland, a gifted young winger, was briefly a sensation before being sold to Manchester City. Only two players, Billy Lake - who remains the club's second-highest scorer, and defender Jimmy Baker, made a successful transition into the Storer era.

Few new managers have ever been so utterly vindicated as Harry Storer was in signing Clarrie Bourton and Jock Lauderdale. Bourton had been displaced at Blackburn where he scored 37 goals in 63 League games, four of them in a 7-5 win at Bramall Lane on 3 March 1930. Lauderdale, who served his apprenticeship in Scotland, had made only a fleeting impression at Blackpool. These two enabled Coventry to become one of the deadliest scoring teams in League football. Bourton was the League's top scorer in his first season, with 49 goals.

City rose to sixth by the end of the 1932/33 season. A side capable of scoring seven goals in the first half, as against Q.P.R, could afford to be occasionally generous in defence.

When lowly Bristol City came to Highfield Road for the penultimate game of the 1933/34 season, the Bantams were destined to finish as runners-up. Promotion hopes had been dashed the previous Saturday at Norwich, which is probably why Bristol City's visit attracted only 7,035 people, the lowest home crowd of the season.

Prior to the match, Bourton had scored 110 goals in 107 League games for Coventry and Lauderdale 44 in 121. When Bourton was injured during the season, the club turned to Arthur Bacon. Bacon scored 16 goals in 14 games, 9 of them in 2 consecutive matches. He was subsequently partially blinded in an accident, and later killed serving as a special constable during an air raid on Derby.

Above: Harry Storer
in later years.

Right: Clarrie Bourton.

In the Bristol City goal, Ken Scattergood saved his team from greater humiliation. Wales international Leslie Jones, who had been signed from Cardiff in January, opened the scoring after 5 minutes, and goals from Lauderdale and Bourton put the Bantams three up after 15 minutes. Frank White and Bourton made it five by half-time. There were further goals from Jones, Bourton (two) and White in the second half. Poor Bristol City missed a penalty two minutes from time.

Clarence Frederick Thomas Bourton was himself a Bristolian. He also died in the area. Bourton served Bristol City as player and manager and behind the scenes over many years. Even Harry Storer could not have expected his first signing to become such a phenomenon. Bourton was the epitome of the strong, old-fashioned centre forward and by far the most consistent goalscorer ever to represent Coventry City.

COVENTRY CITY v. TORQUAY UNITED

2 May 1936
Highfield Road
Football League Division Three (South)
Coventry City 2 Torquay United 1

	P	W	D	L	F	A	W	D	L	F	A	GA	P
1 Coventry City	41	18	1	1	73	11	5	8	8	27	33	2.2727	55
2 Luton Town	41	13	6	2	56	20	9	5	6	25	25	1.8000	55

It is likely that the outcome of this match owed more than to the usual balance of sporting luck and judgement. One of the Coventry directors, Erle Shanks, revealed years later that both the opposition and the referee had, as he put it, 'been squared'. Nonetheless, City still made heavy weather of winning this, their last match, to make sure of promotion.

Midway through the second half, the Torquay left-back, Lew Tapp, duly brought down George McNestry. But McNestry, City's normally reliable penalty-taker, made a hash of things, striking the kick straight at Percy Maggs in the Torquay goal. Fifteen minutes from the end, Torquay actually took the lead when, as a result of a City error, Les Dodds broke down the left and crossed to Ted Lowery. Lowery's shot, fortunately or unfortunately, went in off a post.

Coventry had started the game ahead of Luton on goal average. The two teams had just played each other twice over the previous weekend, the original home fixture having been postponed. Both matches were drawn. The record crowd of 42,975 at Highfield Road on the Monday (it was not even Easter) comfortably beat the previous record of 31,673 for the Sunderland Cup-tie in 1930. There were hundreds locked outside. The Bantams had pulled back to equalise at Kenilworth Road, despite a bad knee injury early in the game to skipper George Mason. City were already without Leslie Jones who had broken his arm three weeks before. Mason missed the last two matches and spent the Torquay game nervously pacing around Gosford Green, racing back to the ground when he heard the roar of the crowd at the final whistle.

Only one team could go up, and Luton were drawing at Q.P.R. Three minutes after Torquay scored, another penalty was awarded, this time for a handling offence. City made sure not to spurn the chance. Acting skipper Ernie Curtis decided to take the kick and blasted the ball low to Maggs' left. The Bantams, who had spent most of the game camped in the Torquay half, took heart, and 3 minutes from time scored the winner. Fred Liddle made a great run on the left, beat right-back Freddie Green and dribbled along the goalline before slipping the ball to Clarrie Bourton who scored unchallenged. It was Bourton's 24th League goal of the season. Luton's 0-0 draw at Q.P.R. proved incidental: the Bantams were champions. There were 30,514 fans in the ground amid scenes not repeated until 1963, by which time the flurry of rattles and trilbies had melted into history.

Sunderland, the First Division champions, were the only side in the League to exceed Coventry's 102 goals. City had scored 502 League goals in just five seasons. At home in 1935/36, they beat Newport 7-1, Millwall 5-0, Brighton 5-0, Crystal Palace 8-1, Q.P.R. 6-1, Cardiff 5-1 and Notts County 5-1. It is little wonder the talk was of 'The Old Five'. The expression was actually derived from the former nickname for Foleshill Great Heath. The Bantams were also winners of the Southern Section Cup, for members of the Third Division (South). They beat Swindon Town 3-2 in the final at Highfield Road. For all that – and another brace from Bourton – City still lost at Midland League Scunthorpe in the FA Cup.

Above: Coventry City, Third Division (South) Champions, 1935/36.

Right: George Mason.

The team had been strengthened during the summer by the signing of two wingers, Arthur Fitton of Preston and George McNestry of Bristol Rovers. In the New Year, the club accepted the offer of an interest-free loan of £3,000 from the *Evening Telegraph* in order to bolster the team during its promotion push, and full-back Jack Astley was signed from Brentford.

City finished the previous season, 1934/35, third in the table. George Mason established himself as the titan at centre half he was to remain for fifteen years and as one of the true giants in the club's history. If it had not been for the war, his 2 unofficial caps for England might have been full international honours. Leslie Jones finished that same season as top scorer ahead of Bourton. He and McNestry then both scored 19 goals during the promotion campaign. Another famous Coventry figure, Billy Frith, was now established in the defence.

It was the culmination of a period under Walter Brandish and Harry Storer as chairman and manager in which the club achieved a rare stability. Notwithstanding the circumstances of the Torquay game, it was a tragedy that Brandish, to whom so much of this revival was due, did not live long enough to see the club promoted for the first time.

Newcastle United v. Coventry City

4 February 1939
St James' Park
Football League Division Two
Newcastle United 0 Coventry City 4

'If it hadn't been for the war...' For those of us born in the years immediately after the end of the Second World War and learning to comprehend adult conversation for the first time during the 1950s, this condition seemed regularly to preface our parents' conversations. We grew up with this oceanic event, this experience – of horror and heroism, of brief encounters and severed aspirations – staring over our shoulders. The shore that was left behind on the other side belonged to a different world, a different time. Memories of our childhood are dotted with bomb sites and the skyscrapers and shopping centres that were beginning to sprout from them.

If it had not been for the war, Coventry City would have got to the First Division thirty years sooner. Such is the myth. The club finished fourth in the Second Division in 1938 and 1939 and many supporters reflected that a turning point had been reached in November 1937 with the transfer of Leslie Jones to Arsenal. Bobby Davidson, a skilful Scottish inside forward who came to Coventry as part of the deal, did not entirely fulfil expectations. City had gone off like a bomb at the start of the 1937/38 campaign and were unbeaten in their first 15 matches. However, something had changed. The buccaneering style of the early 1930s had given way, partly out of necessity, to a more defensive approach. Goalkeeper Bill Morgan and the full-back and half-back lines of Jack Astley and Walter Metcalf, Billy Frith, George Mason and Jack Archer, were for a time almost permanent fixtures.

City had finished eighth in their first season back in the Second Division, with Clarrie Bourton and Jock Lauderdale a fading act. It was the failure to adequately replace both them and Jones that was ultimately to scupper City's hopes of promotion. The egregious Jackie Brown, top scorer in 1936/37 and 1937/38, was sold to Birmingham after an 'unfortunate incident' in the toilets of a Coventry ballroom, when he was caught with his trousers down other than for the customary purpose.

Perhaps the club should have shown more willingness to strengthen the team in its drive for promotion. It is possible that the directors were so unaccustomed to the club's increased financial stability that they were too cautious. Certainly there was a growing degree of scepticism among supporters about real commitment to success and attendances were down by a quarter in 1938/39.

There had been other developments. A new main stand was constructed in 1936. Later in the same year, Sir John Siddeley, chairman of Armstrong-Siddeley, loaned £20,000 to enable the club to purchase the freehold of the Highfield Road ground from the Mercers Company.

In 1937, complaints in the *Evening Telegraph* about the 'scruffy' appearance of the team prompted a change of strip. Storer's reaction was characteristic: 'If I thought a pansy in the middle of the shirt would help to win a match, I would have one on each side. Our players go onto the field to win matches, not to look like matinée idols.'

City were in good nick when they travelled to St James' Park in February 1939. These were fallow years for Newcastle United who had been relegated from the First Division in 1934. The Depression, however, did not undermine their support. By the time Coventry made the trip in the middle of that last winter before the war, there was a crowd of 43,443 to welcome them. The Magpies were in a run of 6 consecutive League matches without scoring. Despite hiccups on either side of Christmas Day, City had won 8 out of their previous 10 games. For the last time before the

After the Blitz.

war, 'The Old Five' had been invoked the previous week against Nottingham Forest. Tom Crawley momentarily looked as if he might at last step into the boots of Bourton with 7 goals in 4 games. Despite their form, the Bantams still contrived an humiliating Cup exit at Chester.

Another brace from Crawley and goals from Davidson and George Taylor gave City a comfortable win that afternoon at Newcastle. Promotion was very much on the cards but a run of only 2 goals in the next 7 games put paid to it.

As manager of Coventry City, Harry Storer straddled the 1930s like a colossus. He was still playing First Division football at Burnley when he accepted the Coventry post. Although he was a thirty-three-year-old entering management with a club which had spent twelve years doing little more than just hanging on, the fans expected tangible achievement from him. It demanded enormous authority from one so young. Did Storer cultivate that fearsome persona to compensate for his youthfulness or had Walter Brandish picked him because of it? Whatever the case, Storer was soon scaring the pants off players of any age. When the young Harry Barratt was left sprawling with an injury at West Ham, it evoked little sympathy. 'Get up, sonny, if you want to continue playing for me,' snarled Storer. Storer stories are legion. Barratt recalled:

> I remember that he used to give us twenty questions on away trips. He'd always beat us, but there was one occasion when Billy Frith and I had got nineteen right and the twentieth question was about Calvary. He wanted to know on which side of Christ did they crucify the thief. We thought about it and then realised we couldn't win. Whatever answer we gave, the Governor would say it was wrong. And that's what happened. We guessed that the thief was hung on Christ's right-hand side. 'You know, Frithy, that's bloody hard luck. He was on the left,' replied Storer.

Thieves were gathering over Europe. The brooks were frozen, the airports almost deserted, and snow disfigured the public statues. The next season came to a halt almost as soon as it started. Who dared guess how far the ocean beyond would spread?

COVENTRY CITY v. SHEFFIELD WEDNESDAY

19 April 1952
Highfield Road
Football League Division Two
Coventry City 0 Sheffield Wednesday 2

	P	W	D	L	F	A	W	D	L	F	A	GA	P
16 Notts County	40	10	5	5	40	27	5	1	14	25	40	0.9701	36
17 Bury	40	12	2	6	40	21	2	5	13	24	44	0.9846	35
18 Barnsley	39	8	6	6	38	32	3	6	10	17	34	0.8333	34
19 Coventry City	40	9	5	6	36	31	5	1	14	22	46	0.7532	34
20 Hull City	40	10	5	5	40	22	1	6	13	15	47	0.7971	33
21 Swansea Town	40	9	4	7	41	25	1	8	11	24	49	0.8784	32
22 Queens Park Rangers	39	7	8	5	34	35	2	4	13	14	42	0.6234	30

It was a new age. Winston Churchill stood at the bottom of the steps to greet the vulnerable figure of Elizabeth as she descended from the aeroplane. The King was dead and this was the first glimpse the newsreels would relay of the new Queen on her return from Kenya.

Coventry City were also reaching the end of an era. Highfield Road had been hit three times during air raids, and a bomb crater in the pitch needed to be filled in. At the end of the war, Harry Storer left to become manager of Birmingham. Storer was replaced by his assistant, Dick Bayliss, whose reign was unexpectedly cut short. Driving back from a scouting mission in Scotland during the great freeze of 1947, he was marooned in a snowstorm on the Yorkshire Moors. His already delicate health was aggravated and he died in April of a kidney complaint at the age of forty-seven.

After the seven lost seasons, there was still a recognisable skeleton to the Coventry team, with George Mason at its heart. Some players, such as Harry Barratt, George Lowrie and Ted Roberts, had appeared briefly before the war. Barratt was later to be a worthy successor to Mason as captain and Roberts scored 75 goals for City after the resumption. Lowrie's goals earned him caps for Wales before his transfer to Newcastle in 1948 for the vast sum of £18,500. Dick Mason and Peter Murphy were prominent among the new faces along with signings such as Don Dearson, Norman Lockhart, Jimmy Alderton, Jimmy McIntosh and Noel Simpson.

City's outside left in 1946/47 was Emilio Aldecoa, the first Spaniard to play in the English League. Aldecoa was one of 4,000 Basque refugee children to have fled to England in the wake of the Spanish Civil War. When he returned to Spain, he won two titles with Barcelona.

City enjoyed two reasonable seasons but by November 1948 they were in the relegation zone. Billy Frith, who had taken up the reins from Bayliss, was sacked. It heralded the return of the talismanic Storer. Storer had mellowed but there is a story of Teddy Davison, the Sheffield United manager, phoning him on the Monday morning after City had won at Bramall Lane and saying: 'You have got nine of the nastiest, dirtiest players I have ever seen on a football pitch. My chairman wants to know what you are going to do about it.' Storer retorted: 'Sack the other two!' Davison, in quiet admiration, asked how Storer succeeded in getting so much commitment from his players, and the Coventry manager confided: 'Listen Teddy, they are more afraid of me than any eleven you put out against them.'

The board backed Storer with money to buy Martin McDonnell, Bryn Allen and Ken Chisholm, who helped put City top of the table by Christmas 1950. The Bantams finished seventh in 1950/51 but an ageing team then began to struggle. Despite the return of Lowrie and the signings of Roy Kirk and the free-scoring Eddie Brown, City were in deep trouble when they came to entertain Sheffield Wednesday in their last home match of the 1951/52 season.

Brown's background was a little surprising. He had entered St Joseph's Theological College in South London, and become known as 'Brother John'. George Smith, visiting St Joseph's in his role as an FA coach, said to Brown: 'I don't know what sort of priest you'll make mate, but you are a born footballer.' Brother John signed for Preston.

City had lost at Hillsborough in December. In his autobiography, Derek Dooley describes George Mason playing one of his last games for City that day:

He was never a man to mince his words. He turned and swore, telling me exactly what he was going to do with me. If he had carried out his threat I might not have been able to walk off the field at the end of the game. However, when the final whistle blew he put an arm round my shoulder and said with a smile, 'Well done, kid.'

Harry Barratt told of a game at Villa Park:

It had been raining all day. The previous week we had weighed the ball at the start and it was 15oz. When we came off, it weighed 27oz. It was near the end of the game at Villa and the ball was saturated again. Eric Houghton was preparing to take a free-kick and I was called into the wall. George Mason grabbed me by the arm and said: 'Stand fast, men – and I hope for Christ it hits you Barratt.'

It did and it had the same effect as a stun grenade. Barratt was poleaxed and recalled: 'Ten seconds later, I was still coughing on the deck and Mason ran up and shouted: "Get up. We ain't cleared it yet."'

Mason himself recalled being summoned to Storer's office later in the 1951/52 season. 'We have had everything we can get out of you. You're knackered and I'm going to give you a free transfer,' said Storer. Mason reflected: 'He was right, of course, but it still hurt. I just broke down and cried.'

Goalkeeper Billy Gilbert reported for the Sheffield Wednesday game with a shoulder injury so Storer had to throw in Derek Spencer at the last minute. Within 90 seconds, the 36,331 crowd was watching Spencer picking the ball out of the net. Dooley had run onto a through ball from Jackie Sewell and smashed it home with a right-foot shot. At the other end of the game, Dooley flicked another through ball past Spencer, and could yet have had a hat-trick but for a brilliant save by the young 'keeper. Sheffield Wednesday left the field as champions. No one had played a bigger part in their success than the twenty-two-year-old goalscoring sensation. He finished the season with 46 goals from 30 league games. Ten months later, tragedy was to supervene. On 14 February 1953, Dooley broke his right leg at Preston. An infection led to gangrene and amputation. The tragedy could have been even greater.

City went to Leeds the following week with the relegation places still to be decided. The story goes that they found themselves lunching at the same hotel as Hull City. Hull saved themselves with a win at Doncaster, but Coventry, with only Q.P.R. below them, lost 3-1 at Elland Road. The Bantams were down. It took a decade for them to re-emerge as the Sky Blues.

HUDDERSFIELD TOWN v. COVENTRY CITY

8 January 1955
Leeds Road
FA Cup Third Round
Huddersfield Town 3 Coventry City 3

Few fans listening on the wireless to the Third Round Cup draw on 13 December 1954 would yet have heard of the likes of Real Madrid. Football belonged at home. The FA Cup to the English was like the World Series has remained to the Americans.

Huddersfield Town were still among the most impressive names in football and Coventry, who had knocked out Northampton and Scunthorpe, were drawn against them. Less than thirty years before, Huddersfield were the mightiest club in England. By the time City visited Leeds Road for a First Division match in 1971 the kit manager had forgotten that a change strip was necessary and City had to borrow a set of orange shirts.

Harry Storer returned to manage Coventry in November 1948, saying: 'Coventry is my club. I made a mistake of leaving it once and have regretted it ever since.' He 'resigned' five years later, almost to the day. Storer's departure precipitated the resignation of Erle Shanks as club president. 'In my opinion the board as at present constituted is completely incapable of pulling the club out of its present deplorable position and the sacking of a manager who has given such loyal service cannot possibly overcome the shortcomings of the directors,' said Shanks. At the AGM, shareholders called for the board's resignation, and in April 1954 Shanks was elected chairman. The young Derrick Robins was one of two new directors.

Relegation brought a forty per cent drop in crowds. The club introduced talented youngsters such as Peter Hill, Lol Harvey, Gordon Nutt and Frank Austin and increasingly used the transfer market as a means of balancing the books.

Jack Fairbrother succeeded Storer in January 1954 but a few weeks later there was a terrible tragedy. On 15 February, Fairbrother and his wife moved into a house in Coventry. On 27 February, after City beat Colchester at Highfield Road, the couple went to a Coventry and District League dinner, at which Fairbrother was the guest speaker. After the dinner, they visited an aunt of his in Coventry before returning home. Shortly after going to bed, Isobel Fairbrother got up to go to the bathroom. At the subsequent inquest Fairbrother said:

> I was dozing and then suddenly I heard a terrific bump. My wife was lying at the bottom of the stairs with her head somehow against the front door. I then practically fell down the stairs to get to her. I carried her upstairs. She could not speak to me. She did not put the bathroom or the landing light on because she did not want to wake the kiddies... on the way back she had mistaken the bedroom for the staircase and gone down the staircase.

She died on 7 March without regaining consciousness. Given the set of circumstances, it was noted that the landing was dangerous. The coroner recorded a verdict of 'Accidental Death'.

After only a few months as manager, Fairbrother resigned. In October 1954 he was succeeded in a caretaker capacity by the former City player Charlie Elliott. Elliott, who was at the scene as an auxiliary fireman when the cathedral burned down in 1940, became famous as a cricket umpire, standing in 42 Test matches.

Reg Matthews, Coventry City and England.

In the first round of the Cup at Northampton, Roy Kirk, who had established himself as George Mason's successor at the heart of the defence, scored the only goal. It was an 80 yard clearance from the edge of his own penalty area which looped over the head of the opposition 'keeper. Two months earlier, Kirk distinguished himself against Leyton Orient by scoring 2 own goals in the same match. The Northampton goalkeeper was one of Coventry's great custodians, Alf Wood, whose move to the County Ground turned out to be only a sabbatical.

Wood had been invalided out of the army with spinal meningitis which threatened his career and also prematurely aged him in appearance. Despite it all, he did not miss a single Coventry game between August 1945 and May 1951, and that was in the days when goalkeepers were fair game for the shoulder of any bruiser of a centre forward.

Huddersfield were rated second-favourites to win the Cup but were a goal down to Coventry after only 4 minutes. On a heavily sanded pitch, Eric Johnson, who learned just before the match that he had become a father again, crossed for Tommy Capel to put City ahead. The Bantams kept in front until the 28th minute when Jimmy Glazzard scored the first of two goals. Willie Watson appeared to put the game beyond City's reach when he made it 3-1 after 57 minutes but Coventry fought pluckily and possessed a wonderful goalkeeper in Matthews. Born in Coventry, Reg Matthews remains one of the great figures in the City canon. Brave, agile and boasting a lithesome grace not readily associated with goalkeepers of the time, Matthews became, in 1956, the first Coventry player to win a full England cap. In five internationals he was never on the losing side. Matthews went on to play for Chelsea and Derby but later said: 'Looking back, I don't think I should have left Coventry City... that was where my heart lay.'

Jack Lee pulled a goal back for City after 64 minutes and then, 7 minutes from time, Capel gathered the ball after a misskick, ran through the mud with two Terriers defenders snapping at his heels and smashed the ball home for the equaliser.

The replay was on the following Thursday afternoon. Floodlights had first been used at Highfield Road for a friendly against Queen of the South in 1953, but the first FA Cup-tie ever to be sanctioned under lights did not take place until 1955/56, when Kidderminster Harriers played Brierley Hill Alliance. City took Huddersfield to extra time but lost 2-1. Charlie Elliott was offered the manager's job on a full-time basis but declined it. The following week the club announced the appointment of a new manager to take over in the close season. His identity proved as surprising as it was unexpected.

Coventry City v. King's Lynn

25 November 1961
Highfield Road
FA Cup Second Round
Coventry City 1 King's Lynn 2

The medieval port and market town of King's Lynn has many secrets and delights. As you walk up the aisle of St Nicholas' Chapel for instance, you tread on the name of Robinson Cruso; Daniel Defoe added the letter 'e' to his eponymous hero. You may not readily associate the town with its footballing achievements but in 1961 King's Lynn were playing among the elite of non-league football in the Southern League Premier Division. Despite relegation at the end of the season, the Linnets enjoyed a memorable Cup run; victories at Dulwich Hamlet and Chelmsford City, two of the weightier names in non-league football, earned a trip to Coventry in the second round.

'You can't give players something that they don't possess. You can't talk to them and try to kid them. But if the ability and fight is not there you can do *nothing* about it. I'm very disappointed.' That was the reaction of Harry Barratt, the former Coventry skipper, quoted in the *Daily Herald*. He was talking as manager of Gillingham after his side's 2-0 defeat at Highfield Road in the first round. Billy Frith could have said much the same about his Coventry players after the second round. The name of King's Lynn, more even than Sutton United, continues to resonate in Coventry to this day.

Amid a flickering of flashbulbs in January 1955, Coventry City appointed Jesse Carver as manager. Carver had become one of the most successful coaches in Italy and had taken Juventus to the Italian title. However, despite being paid a king's ransom at Coventry, he soon decamped and returned to Italy to manage Lazio. Carver was succeeded by his assistant, George Raynor, who was between spells, winning the Olympic gold medal in 1948 and reaching the World Cup Final in 1958, as national team coach to Sweden. Raynor, who rarely saw eye-to-eye with the board and was replaced by Harry Warren in June 1956, wrote: 'I admire football-minded businessmen who climb the social ladders, but I detest those people who use football purely as the ladder'. The continental methods, that for a while made Coventry a distinctive if not very successful side, were dropped, but the cosmopolitan flame continued briefly to burn with Steve Mokone.

Mokone, the first black player to appear for Coventry, was the first black South African footballer to play professionally in Europe. The long-ball style did not suit him and he played only 4 games, but he later had short spells with Cardiff City and Barnsley. 'Kalamazoo' left Coventry for Heracles, a club in the small Dutch town of Almelo. The legend of *De Zwarte Meteoor* (The Black Meteor) and the dribbling skills and pace with which he transformed a struggling team, are immortalised in book and film, and emblazoned throughout Almelo. He went on to enjoy several seasons in Serie A with Torino. Mokone and his wife and daughter then moved to the USA where he gained a doctorate, and became an assistant professor of psychiatry. He won a bitter custody battle for his daughter but was accused of violent assault on his wife. Mokone maintained his innocence but was convicted and served eight years. In a letter to the New York Supreme Court in 1984, Desmond Tutu wrote of 'a gentle man. He speaks for kindness and compassion among humans.' Subsequent research strongly suggested that Mokone, who had pre-existing ties to the ANC and had become increasingly political in America, was framed. Mokone later served as a goodwill ambassador for the South African tourist board in New York and helped found a charitable institution that assisted young South Africans with a talent for sport in finding places in further education.

'If you want a cathedral,
we've got one to spare'.

Morale at Highfield Road was at its lowest ebb in the summer of 1957 when twenty-one players asked for a transfer. The chairman, Erle Shanks, had not ingratiated himself by taking over the front page of the programme to announce that 'unfortunately some of our players have not always given of their best'. Winger Alan Moore was suspended for 'gross insubordination', the nature of which, one imagines, was of rather fewer syllables.

The 1957/58 season began with the sacking of Warren and ended with the resignation of Shanks. Billy Frith became manager for a second spell and Walter Brandish Jnr took over as chairman. Almost from the start, it had become a relegation struggle for most teams in the Third Divisions North and South. This was on account of the decision actually proposed by Coventry, to form a Fourth Division out of the lower halves of the two sections. City failed to make the cut. However, promotion gained at the first attempt served to restore some optimism. Ray Straw – whose aggregate of 85 goals was only substantially bettered in the club's history by Bourton and Lake – was top scorer with 27 goals. Two young defenders by the names of Curtis and Kearns then established themselves in the team and, in November 1958, Frith signed wing half Ronnie Farmer and a brilliant South African goalkeeper, Arthur Lightening, from Nottingham Forest. In 1960, City became the last holders of the Southern Professional Floodlight Cup. The competition was succeeded the following season by the Football League Cup.

Frith's preparations for the King's Lynn tie were hampered by injuries. City looked lethargic and out-of-touch as their opponents exerted all the early pressure, but, after 28 minutes the Bantams broke away and fortuitously took the lead. Peter Hill was tackled by Wilson as he moved through on the right; goalkeeper Manning ran out and Hindle sliced the ball into his own net. Suddenly though, with two goals in the space of 3 minutes, King's Lynn were ahead. Johnson hammered a pass from Wright past Lightening and then Bacon swung over a neat cross for Wright himself to charge in and head the ball home off the underside of the bar. Brian Hill missed an open goal for City before the interval and in a goalmouth scramble later in the game the hosts could yet have scored an undeserved equaliser.

The *Coventry Evening Telegraph* wrote of 'the most grim page in City's modern history' and of 'such puny and deplorably inept resistance.' Derrick Robins, who had been chairman for just over a year, described it as 'an utterly disastrous result for the football club.' Four days later, Billy Frith was sacked along with chief scout Arthur Jepson and trainers Alf Wood and Ted Roberts. Frith carved out a new career as Head of Mathematics at Willenhall Wood School. Goalkeeper Wood, who joined the club in 1935 and came out of retirement to play 12 games in 1958 at the age of forty-three, said: 'We're the victims of results. We have been trying to teach carthorses to be footballers.'

In the third round, King's Lynn lost 4-0 at Everton. The King's Lynn game was not quite the watershed it appeared; who should be sitting in the stand as an unofficial guest of Derrick Robins but Jimmy Hill.

Coventry City v. Sunderland

25 March 1963
Highfield Road
FA Cup Fifth Round
Coventry City 2 Sunderland 1

The Sunderland game became part of Coventry City folklore. If King's Lynn was seen as the catalyst for a revolution, Sunderland was the endorsement. In six days in March 1963, crowds totalling more than 90,000 crammed into Highfield Road for two FA Cup-ties. The old stands had not embraced too many great games in recent years and the ground had only occasionally stretched out for national attention. These two pulsating matches confirmed the new spirit that was sweeping through the corridors.

With the club languishing anonymously in the Third Division, Derrick Robins turned to a seemingly unlikely figure to help it do justice to the city to which it belonged. Jimmy Hill's playing career was already coming to a close when it was ended by injury. Hill, a flamboyant inside forward whose beard went before him, was a member of a distinguished Fulham side promoted to the First Division in 1959. In 1961, as chairman of the Professional Footballers' Association, he became a national figure, successfully campaigning for the abolition of the maximum wage. The players of today owe more to Jimmy Hill than they can imagine. However, by November of that year, he had become a rebel without a cause.

It was at a Lord's Taverners function that Hill and Robins were introduced to each other by the cricketer Jim Laker. Robins invited Hill to his house in the week before the King's Lynn game. It was there that Robins asked him whether he might like to become the manager of Coventry City. Hill had qualified as a coach when he was twenty-four and had performed that role with the Oxford University team. He was ready for a new challenge and he accepted the post the following week despite the King's Lynn fiasco. He was only thirty-three.

The early ripples of the Hill era, with the team finishing fourteenth at the end of 1961/62, betrayed little of the waves to come. By the start of the next season, Hill and Robins had given the club a new coat of paint. Robins made £30,000 of his own money available to rebuild the team. Hill appointed a new backroom staff. There was innovation and inspiration, trial and error – on and off the field. In August 1962, City ran out in a new strip for a friendly at St Andrews. Derek Henderson, doyen of *Coventry Evening Telegraph* football writers, dubbed the team 'The Sky Blues'.

Hill's first signing was Roy Dwight from Gravesend. Dwight, who had broken his leg playing for Nottingham Forest in the 1959 Cup Final, become known later as the uncle of Elton John. At the start of 1962/63, City kicked off with a new forward line: Humphries, Barr, Bly, Whitehouse and Laverick. Both Willie Humphries, a wee winger who proved to be one of Hill's best signings, and Hugh Barr, whose goals had enabled Linfield to carry all before them in the Irish League, were Northern Ireland internationals. Later in the season, Ken Hale from Newcastle took over from Barr. Jimmy Whitehouse, a fair-haired inside forward who arrived on a free-transfer from Reading, wove many an attack during a brief spell at the club. He was replaced by the young Ernie Machin – 'I liked the colour of his eyes,' Hill explained, leading to comments about 'Hill's blue-eyed boy'. Bobby Laverick – one of J.H.'s few failures, who lasted for only 4 games – was replaced by a young winger born in Ystradgynlais, Ronnie Rees. The biggest signing was Terry Bly, whose 52 goals had helped Peterborough into the Third Division at the first attempt. Another important newcomer, signed from Chelsea, was full-back John Sillett.

Jimmy Hill and Derrick Robins.

By Christmas, City were looking confident in the League and well placed for a promotion push. Bournemouth and Millwall, the latter after a replay, were seen off in the Cup. Lincoln were next. It had been unusually mild in December but by the end of the year the whole country was engulfed in snow, in a spell of terrible weather that would become ingrained in the national myth. City's first match of the New Year could not be played until 23 February. Meanwhile, Hill took the team to Dublin to play a friendly against Manchester United. He was not to know that the two teams would be renewing their acquaintance a few weeks later. On 6 March, sixty days and a record sixteen postponements after the match was originally scheduled, City crushed Lincoln 5-1 at Sincil Bank.

The Sky Blues had emerged from their chrysalis. At White Hart Lane, they beat Second Division Portsmouth in a second replay. The fifth round beckoned. This was to be one of the great nights. Never was there such a sense of anticipation and such excitement. Sunderland may only have been a Second Division side – they were to miss out on promotion on goal average – but, apart from Huddersfield in 1955, they were the biggest club to have visited Highfield Road in the League or FA Cup for over a decade. The official attendance was 40,487 but thousands more forced their way in as three of the gates were broken down. There were well over 50,000 people in the ground.

Sunderland took the lead after 33 minutes. The scorer was Johnny Crossan, who had made a triumphant return after three seasons in Holland and Belgium. Crossan's life ban from British football, for accepting expenses as an amateur and asking for a share from a transfer fee, had been commuted.

Coventry kept up the pressure throughout the second half but the noose was inexorably tightening when, eight minutes from time, an equaliser came. The goal itself was a bit of a fluke. Young defender Dietmar Bruck, a local boy born in Danzig, sent in a speculative centre that transfixed Jim Montgomery. It flew over the Sunderland goalkeeper's head, struck the angle and dropped into the net. Three minutes later, City took the lead when George Curtis rose to a cross from John Sillett. It was a combination whose efforts nearly a quarter-of-a-century later would humble even this moment. But it was more than enough for now. The whistle went, the breeches burst. There had never been so much noise. Fans flooded onto the field. Curtis, ever the inspiring captain and personification of his team's spirit, was leaping in the air. The Sky Blue Song – J.H.'s bit of Eton piracy – cut through the spring night, and moments later Sunderland were trooping disconsolately back to the dressing room. Peter Lorenzo, in the *Daily Herald,* had this to say: 'I will remember it as one of the greatest nights in all Cup history – the night a superbly spirited Third Division side came back from almost certain defeat to conquer a Sunderland side of giants'. Coventry City, once a backwater of a club, were dictating the headlines. Highfield Road was bulging in every way.

As if in a letter from Tom Champagne of *Reader's Digest*, the Sky Blues knew what their prize would be before they played the fifth round. Manchester United were still rebuilding from the Munich disaster five years before and struggling in the League, but they lined up with the likes of Law and Charlton – and also Maurice Setters.

On the Wednesday, the day of the publication of Beeching's report into the future of the railways, over 30,000 queued in the pouring rain at Highfield Road. The tickets – a maximum of two per person – sold out in just over three hours. The match attendance was 44,000.

The Sky Blues were a goal up after 5 minutes. In the space of a few days, a club had been transported from relative obscurity to dreamland. Terry Bly, whose goals knocked out Manchester United on the way to taking Third Division Norwich to the semi-finals in 1959, took a knee-high cross from Willie Humphries and his shot flew in off Bill Foulkes. Eleven minutes later, United had a remarkable let-off when the ball spun off two defenders and onto a post.

However, after 27 minutes, the Reds were level with a characteristic volley from Bobby Charlton. Another thunderbolt from Charlton nosed United in front after 49 minutes. Then, with just over an hour gone, Bly appeared to be pushed off the ball. The ball ran loose to Humphries who cracked it home, only for the referee to rule that Bly had handled. Bly hit the post with a tremendous shot but then Bruck and goalkeeper Bob Wesson got in a terrible tangle and Albert Quixall side-footed the ball into an empty net to make it 3. The dream was over.

The Sky Blues' 22-match unbeaten run was at an end. It had been City's sixth cup-tie in less than twenty-five days. Noel Cantwell, who was absent from the Highfield Road game, went on to lift the Cup for Manchester United.

This was not the end of the season's dramas. In April, Jimmy Hill made the most sensational decision of his entire managership. He paid a club-record fee of £21,000 for the Peterborough's' centre forward, George Hudson. Bly, who had scored 30 goals in 42 appearances, only played one more game. Hudson, one of the most accomplished centre forwards ever to play for Coventry, and, incidentally, the only player ever to be sent off playing for Jimmy Hill, scored a hat-trick on his debut. The Hudson in/Bly out debate raged on but Hill judged just the right moment to sell his player. Fixture fatigue took its toll as City finished fourth in the table but one thing was certain: the Sky Blue vision was now inextinguishable.

Coventry City *v.* Manchester United, 30 March 1963.

Highfield Road, 1962.

COVENTRY CITY v. COLCHESTER UNITED

25 April 1964
Highfield Road
Football League Division Three
Coventry City 1 Colchester United 0

	P	W	D	L	F	A	W	D	L	F	A	GA	P
1 Crystal Palace	45	17	4	1	37	11	6	10	7	35	37	1.5000	60
2 Coventry City	45	13	7	2	61	32	8	9	6	36	29	1.5902	58
3 Watford	45	16	6	1	57	28	7	6	9	21	29	1.3684	58

'They've done it!' proclaimed the 'Pink' as City clinched promotion on the last day of the season. The Sky Blues took the Third Division championship by having a goal average 0.1752 better than Crystal Palace. Palace surprisingly lost at home to Oldham. Watford, who had been leading at Luton until losing to 2 late goals by John O'Rourke, finished 2 points behind.

After reaching the quarter-finals of the Cup and finishing fourth in the table, City fans anticipated promotion in 1963/64. The Sky Blues set the pace from the start with a 5-1 home win over Crystal Palace and dropped only one point in the first 7 matches. Highlights included an 8-1 thrashing of Shrewsbury and a 6-3 win at Q.P.R. By early in Januray, City opened up a 9-point gap by early in January. Promotion looked a formality. However, at Reading the following week the team started an 11-match run without a win and, by the middle of February, the lead had dribbled down to a single point. The seeds of doubt were well and truly sown.

The focus for Sky Blues confidence was the finesse of George Hudson. Hudson scored 26 goals by the turn of the year, 10 of them in a purple patch during November, the month of President Kennedy's assassination. But the supply, initially on account of illness and injury, agonisingly dried up. The nadir for the team was a 5-2 home defeat by Southend. Jimmy Hill procured wing half John Smith from Tottenham and the thirty-year-old Southampton centre forward, George Kirby. After defeat at promotion rivals Bournemouth, Kirby scored a hat-trick on 28 March on his home debut. The nightmare was over. Come the penultimate game at Peterborough, City had put together a 6-match unbeaten run. They might have won at Millwall the previous Saturday had it not been for Ronnie Farmer's only ever penalty miss in twenty-three attempts for the club. There were 13,000 visiting fans at London Road but the Sky Blues lost 2-0. Promotion hung in the balance but Brentford scraped a draw at Watford the following night, so beating Colchester would see City home.

Attendances stick in the mind like cricketers' initials. The figure of 36,901 for the Colchester game, the largest League attendance at Highfield Road since Christmas 1949, is as redolent for some as M.J.K. The manager ordered his players to take sleeping pills on the two nights before the game and brought in the comedian Jimmy Tarbuck to crack a few jokes in the dressing room.

The talking point during the week was the likely recall of Hudson. The unthinkable had happened when Hill dropped him after the Bournemouth defeat. In the first half against Colchester, he and Willie Humphries carved huge gaps in the U's defence, and it was no surprise when City took the lead after 24 minutes. A left-wing cross from Ronnie Rees was whipped into the net by Hudson for only his second goal of the year. Colchester, managed by Neil Franklin, were second best for much of the game. Hudson was suffering from cramp for most of the second half and went off for attention. His return coincided with a great cheer which had spread like a Mexican wave

Coventry City. Third Division Champions. 1963/64. From left to right, back row: Hugh Barr, George Hudson, John Sillett, Bob Wesson, Dave Meeson, Mick Kearns, Ronnie Farmer, Brian Hill. Middle row: Willie Humphries, Ken Hale, George Curtis, George Kirby, John Mitten, Ronnie Rees. Front row: Graham Newton, Dietmar Bruck.

from the press box. Within seconds, the loudspeaker announcement from cricketer Godfrey Evans was that Watford and Palace had both lost. In those days, Coventry kicked off at 3.15 p.m. Not for the last time was a City side relieved to play out time in the knowledge of other results.

In the early 1960s, when the pall of Woodbines and social servility began to lift, football clubs were slow to engage with the new generation; Derrick Robins was one of the first to grasp the need. In the hard-sell of today, the extent to which Robins and Hill sought to harness public enthusiasm cannot be overestimated. Autograph sessions with free pop and crisps may not sound much, but in 1961 it made headline news. It was Coventry City who then took the lead with the Sky Blue Special (a charter train to away fixtures), Radio Sky Blue, closed-circuit television relays, the Sky Blue Pool, Sky Blue Rose (Rose McNulty, the ClubCall voice of her day), matchday magazines and even a restaurant good enough to boast a Michelin star. In the opening paragraph of his 1968 book, *The Sky Blues*, Derek Henderson wrote:

> In an age of so much vision and enterprise in other fields, British football needs clubs like Coventry City. Not for nothing have they been saturated with unprecedented publicity. They are the most written about, and certainly one of the most talked-about clubs of the 1960s.

Robins, a stockbroker's son from Bexleyheath, established a successful pre-fabricated concrete buildings business in Banbury. He became a great patron of English cricket. Having played 2 games behind the wicket for for Warwickshire in 1947, he made the next of his 3 remaining first-class appearances twenty-two years later, captaining his own international eleven against the West Indies at the age of nearly fifty-five. The D.H. Robins XI was a regular feature in the 1970s, both in England and on tour abroad.

Some things though eluded even Derrick Robins. In 1973, at the time he made way for his son Peter as Coventry chairman, he was not alone in saying: 'TV should be banned except for the Cup Final and internationals.'

Only hours after the Colchester game, the old stand on the Thackhall Street side of the ground was demolished to make way for the completion of the new Sky Blue Stand. With promotion, Coventry City had at last returned from the wilderness. The first part of the Sky Blue revolution was complete.

COVENTRY CITY v. QUEENS PARK RANGERS

13 April 1965
Highfield Road
Football Combination Division Two
Coventry City 1 Queens Park Rangers 0

Reserve team football has always played a more significant role in England than elsewhere, and in the 1960s it was still at its peak. In the days of the magic sponge, when no Cup Final was complete without at least one player writhing with cramp, running took precedence over the more fastidious refinements of diet and fitness we acknowledge today. If you were not required for first-team duty, you had a run-out in the stiffs the same afternoon. Clubs did not need to take a bench-load of twelfth-men to matches in those days; substitutes were only introduced in 1965/66.

Apart from the Cup Final and England v. Scotland, there was hardly any live football yet on television. 'They think it's all over' was a year away and *Match of the Day* had only started that season. Despite the success of Coventry's Sky Blue Special, it was less common for fans to travel long distances to away matches. Large numbers of supporters, starved of any football on the telly, went along to watch the Reserves.

Highfield Road had never attracted such a large crowd for a reserve fixture. The record stood at over 10,000 for a pre-war game against Arsenal. For Q.P.R., whose average home gate in the Third Division was only 5,670, the turnout of 12,132 to watch their reserves must have come as a bit of a surprise. Coventry were pushing for promotion to Division One of the Football Combination. Jimmy Hill drafted in Allan Harris, Brian Hill, Ronnie Rees and David Clements from Saturday's first team. In those days, the Reserves was not seen as a forum for untried kids. Promising youngsters had to earn their place. Bobby Gould, an eighteen-year-old centre forward who was already taking his first steps on the big stage, was one of these. His 72nd-minute goal proved decisive. *Nemo* reported: 'Rees cut in from the right to deliver a low piledriver which the goalkeeper did well to get down to, but couldn't hold… Gould whipped the ball just inside the left-hand post.'

Only a week before, there had been a crowd of 8,759 for the Luton game. The average attendance in 1964/65 was 4,820. It rose to 6,342 the following season. Even in the 1930s the average had never been so high.

It looked for a time as if City's first team would also be in the running for promotion. The Sky Blues kicked off with 5 consecutive victories but Derby, with Reg Matthews returning to Highfield Road for the first time since his transfer to Chelsea eight years before, beat City on 9 September to signal a run of 5 defeats. The Sky Blues finished the season a satisfactory tenth. There were some high-scoring encounters at home, such as the 5-4 defeat of the eventual champions, Newcastle. There were also contrasting emotions at Highfield Road in the League Cup. Memories of 1963 were evoked when Sunderland, now in the First Division, were beaten 4-2 but City crashed 8-1 to Leicester in the quarter-finals.

David Clements was one of two newcomers who were to play a major part. The nineteen-year-old Ulsterman scored in 8 of his first 10 matches. Bill Glazier, signed – rather aptly – from Crystal Palace, was the other. At £35,000, Glazier was the most expensive goalkeeper in the world. The quality of his performances soon established him in the England Under-23s, but a badly broken leg, sustained at Maine Road on Easter Monday, put his career on hold and ended any hopes of his making the World Cup squad.

George Hudson.

In 1968 Coventry City joined the Central League, the northern brother of the Football Combination. City, who became the southernmost members, recognised that it was a stronger league. The opening fixture resulted in a 2-1 defeat at Huddersfield, Mick Kearns scoring the City goal. A crowd of 7,225 watched the first home game, a 2-0 defeat by Sheffield Wednesday. There were 10,302 at Highfield Road to see City gain their first point, against Manchester United, and 7,123 for the next home match. However, the novelty soon wore off and the end of season average dropped to 3,277. City had to wait until their ninth game for their first win, 3-0 at home to Nottingham Forest. Gerry Baker finished that first season as top scorer with 11 goals, and Graham Paddon made 39 appearances.

The Sky Blues were runners-up in the Central League in 1973/74 and 1979/80, both times to Liverpool. In 1974, the margin between the teams was 10 points but, in 1980, City's 23 wins and nine draws left them only a point behind, Liverpool winning 21 and drawing 14. City, who were also leading scorers with 96 goals, would have been champions had there been 3 points for a win. In 1999, the Sky Blues, who had been relegated from the Premier Division of what was now the Pontin's League, finished as First Division champions. After thirty-one seasons, Stefano Gioacchini scored City's last goal before the club left to become founder members of the FA Premier Reserve League.

We are spoiled by satellite nowadays, and consumed by umpteen interests. Sadly, at most grounds, 'The Reserves' has long since lost its sense of occasion. It attracts a dwindling coterie of fans on evenings when the stark, staccato shouts rend the air like distant cries at a dog track.

COVENTRY CITY v. WOLVERHAMPTON WANDERERS

29 April 1967
Highfield Road
Football League Division Two
Coventry City 3 Wolverhampton Wanderers 1

	P	W	D	L	F	A	W	D	L	F	A	GA	P
1 Wolverhampton Wanderers	39	14	4	2	49	19	10	4	5	33	21	2.0500	56
2 Coventry City	39	15	3	1	40	14	6	9	5	27	26	1.6750	54

This match was the culmination of five extraordinary years. The city of Coventry needed, not for the first or last time, to rediscover an identity as it rebuilt from the ravages of the Second World War. By the 1960s, the motor industry was booming, unemployment was low. The new shopping precinct, angular and functional as befitted the architecture of the time, spoke of a new assurance and prosperity. Visitors flocked to the heart of England to behold Basil Spence's bold new cathedral and to celebrate Shakespeare's 400th birthday. Meanwhile, for many, the focal point became the performance of their local football team. Jimmy Hill and Derrick Robins were as vibrant and forceful a pairing as any in English football. They fostered a sense of identity with the community as they broke the game free from the shell of austerity. Hill, having played a critical role in enabling footballers to make a proper living for themselves, awakened soccer to a relevance beyond the back page. And in a sky-blue vapour of publicity, he and Robins determined on Division One.

The Bantams had finished fourth in the two seasons before the war, but in 1965/66 the Sky Blues went one better. City won their last match at promotion rivals Huddersfield to put them second to Manchester City. However, with Southampton having 2 games left to play, celebrations were muted. Forty-eight hours later, the Saints drew at relegated Leyton Orient and only needed to avoid an avalanche of goals at Maine Road to be promoted. The result was 0-0 and City finished third. The Sky Blues, however, could look back on a 5-1 win against Southampton at Highfield Road in which George Hudson scored one of the great Coventry City goals. Hudson, with his back to goal, flicked the ball over Tony Knapp's head before turning and nonchalantly heading it past the 'keeper. Not surprisingly, the sale of Hudson, for whom the bustling Bobby Gould was the ready but raw replacement, was a major controversy. For the fans, it was like having a dummy snatched from the mouth. In a fit of pique, droves of them abandoned City to attend Hudson's debut for Northampton but Hill – as usual – had got it right.

Coventry had come tantalisingly close to promotion. There was a ticklish sense of anticipation as 20 August approached, in the wake too of England's World Cup triumph. International football's monopoly of our attention that July stimulated the erroneous idea that the domestic football season gets longer, whereas it is actually the cricket season that continues to grow.

City's season started fairly well but wobbled badly at the beginning of October. Defeat at Preston was followed by a midweek trip to Brighton for a League Cup-tie and then the long haul to Carlisle. City lost in Cumberland and Hill made Ian Gibson, his record signing that summer, the scapegoat. It seemed strange that part of the reason Hill was criticising Gibson was for the dribbling game which was his particulat forte. The two had a much-publicised squabble and Gibson was transfer-listed. City lost the Brighton replay but then put their game together with good results against Blackburn and Bolton. During the same week, in Aberfan, childhood innocence was lost forever in the horror that smothered Pantglas Junior School.

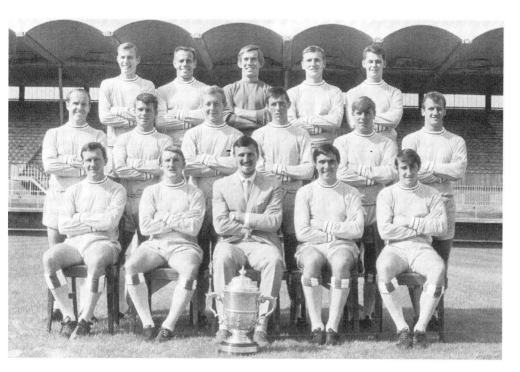

Coventry City, Second Division Champions. 1966/67. From left to right, back row: Brian Lewis, George Curtis, Bill Glazier, Mick Kearns, Dudley Roberts. Middle row: Ronnie Farmer, Dietmar Bruck, John Tudor, Mick Coop, Ernie Machin, Brian Hill. Front row: John Key, Ian Gibson, Jimmy Hill, Bobby Gould, Ronnie Rees. Abesnt: David Clements.

The Sky Blue Song turned shrill at successive defeats by Crystal Palace and Huddersfield. Hill decided to restore Gibson for the Cardiff game. Gibbo, puggish in appearance and sullen in his craft and art, was an inventive juggler. His career – like that of Blackpool's Tony Green, his rival for potential Scotland honours – became dogged by injuries. On that November afternoon, Gibson's two goals set the Sky Blues on a 25-match unbeaten run that was to see them into the First Division.

The heroics of Bill Glazier helped City gain victory at Wolves, still a resonant name from a decade before. This was followed by a 5-0 home win against leaders Ipswich. Bobby Gould, the local boy whose determination characterised the spirit of the team, scored his first hat-trick.

City lost 4-3 to Newcastle in the Cup but continued to squeeze out points in the League. By the end of March, Gould's winner at rivals Blackburn proved decisive. Two wins and three draws followed. On 25 April, Bolton went to Ewood Park and drew. Blackburn could no longer catch us: we were up.

Whom did the fixture list thrown up for the following Saturday at Highfield Road but Wolves, who had also won promotion. The fever of the game swept the population.

The official attendance at Highfield Road was 51,455 but in truth the crowd was much bigger than that, pushing back the boundaries of possibility as the team had done. The ground record, against Aston Villa, had stood at 44,930 since 1938. Highfield Road was swollen with humanity, from the bulging Spion Kop downwards. Every vantage point was exploited with people on the stand roofs and many others straddling the girders of the floodlight pylons like decorations on a Christmas tree. Police quietly allowed those at the front of the crowd, mostly youngsters, to spill over onto the track.

Gould, out of the side with a broken thumb, was replaced by John Tudor. City kicked off from the Spion Kop end and forced a first-minute corner. From the clearance, Ernie Hunt – who less than a year later would be wearing sky blue – broke away to win a corner for Wolves. After only 9 minutes, Derek Dougan found his way into the referee's book as a result of some early sparks with George Curtis. Wolves looked menacing in breakaways but it was City who came closest to scoring 5 minutes before half-time when Tudor moved onto a pass from Ernie Machin and fired into the side netting. Almost immediately, Wolves took the lead when Curtis could only push the ball out to Dougan whose flick-on was driven home by Peter Knowles.

Wolves had dominated the play but Gibbo was beginning to take control, bringing inspiration to bear on City's industriousness. On the hour, Machin cracked home an equaliser from the edge of the box after Ronnie Rees had burst forward on a run from his own half. Suddenly, there were hundreds of jubilant young fans on the pitch. Four minutes later, City swept downfield again with Tudor feeding Gibson. Gibson's shot struck a defender and deflected past Phil Parkes and into the net. Once more there was a pitch invasion and this time the referee had an announcement made that any further encroachment would force him to abandon the game.

Wolves had lost all their first-half coolness and were being given the runaround. Mick Kearns had to head off his line but within a few seconds it was 3-1. Machin passed to Gibson, who held the ball for a moment before flicking it sideways for Rees to hammer a drive into the far corner.

Ernie Machin scores City's first goal despite Ernie Hunt's tackle.

Highfield Road,
29 April 1967.

Supporters, in a miracle of self-control, held back for 5 more minutes. Hill and Robins saluted the crowd, J.H. leading a chorus of the Sky Blue Song. It had been the greatest day in the club's history.

With 2 games to go, Wolves were still top, but only on goal average. They went on to defeat Norwich and City drew at Ipswich. In the final game, the Sky Blues beat Millwall 3-1 at Highfield Road whilst Wolves lost 4-1 at Crystal Palace. Coventry City were champions.

Over 25,000 had turned out in the week of the Millwall game to salute George Curtis and Mick Kearns in their testimonial match against Liverpool. Curtis, unearthed from Snowdown Colliery in Kent, and the Nuneaton-born Kearns, played 916 first-team games between them for the club.

City's success owed a lot to the strong spine of the team. Like a woodpecker at a tree, Bill Glazier indented the goal-posts with the nervous tapping of his boots before set-pieces. In an era of outstanding English goalkeepers, his consistency placed him above almost all the rest. Curtis, the Iron Man with the defiant chest, stood behind a belligerent young Bobby Gould at centre forward, while Gibson pulled the strings. Above all, this was an achievement of teamwork, fitness and determination. Along with Curtis and Kearns, Brian Hill went on to play in all four divisions for City as did Ronnie Farmer who gave way later in the season to Brian Lewis. There was Machin, Rees and Tudor, the experienced winger John Key, David Clements – continuing his versatile education next to Curtis – and Dietmar Bruck. Most important was the motivating skill and personality of a very shrewd manager.

Flattering and encouraging things were said about the Sky Blues as they looked forward to taking their place in the First Division. There was a suspicion that the team was slightly short of class and would need to consolidate. However, Coventry City had big aspirations.

It was inconceivable that Curtis would be torn from the team so soon in August, let alone that J.H. could be leaving us to face this brave new world on our own.

SOUTHAMPTON v. COVENTRY CITY

11 May 1968
The Dell
Football League Division One
Southampton 0 Coventry City 0

	P	W	D	L	F	A	W	D	L	F	A	GA	P
18 Sheffield Wednesday	42	6	10	5	32	24	5	2	14	19	39	0.8095	34
19 Coventry City	41	8	5	8	32	32	1	9	10	19	39	0.7183	32
20 Sheffield United	41	7	4	9	24	29	4	6	11	24	39	0.7059	32
21 Stoke City	40	9	3	8	28	28	4	3	13	20	44	0.6667	32
22 Fulham	41	6	4	11	27	41	4	3	13	28	52	0.5914	27

This draw, along with Sheffield United's home defeat by Chelsea, secured City a second season in the top flight. It had been a difficult and traumatic baptism. Never again should such a struggle be allowed to occur.

Coventry's debut in the First Division got off to the worst possible start. Jimmy Hill had resigned days before the start of the campaign. The club was not prepared to meet his demand for a ten-year contract, and London Weekend Television and *The Big Match* beckoned with a challenge which J.H. found irresistible. In the second match, George Curtis' leg was broken by a bad tackle from Nottingham Forest's Frank Wignall.

Derrick Robins was on the verge of appointing Malcolm Allison as Hill's successor. He and Allison had a verbal agreement but a furious Robins withdrew the offer when news of it was leaked to a national newspaper. At this point, Matt Busby phoned Robins and commended Noel Cantwell to him. Cantwell was club captain at Old Trafford and reaching the end of an illustrious playing career. Within hours, he was being paraded at Highfield Road as the new manager.

Cantwell depended on the consistency of players such as Bill Glazier. Bobby Gould, whose twenty-four goals helped City to the promised land, was sold to Arsenal and replaced by Sunderland's Neil Martin – a player of sleeker touch, and unmatched in the air by almost any British forward of his generation. The prodigious Willie Carr, barely eighteen years old, brought inspiration to a midfield shorn by injury for much of the season of the mercurial Ian Gibson.

The most influential presence was Cantwell's former Old Trafford team-mate, Maurice Setters. George Curtis had become part of the furniture at Coventry but Setters, a battered chest on gnarled legs, was dug out from Stoke after Tony Knapp failed to fill the gap. It was Setters' leadership, above all, that kept City up.

In March, City enjoyed an intoxicating win over Manchester United. United were top of the League and had just returned from a European Cup quarter-final in Poland. They would bring tears to our eyes with their wonderful victory over Benfica, in the days when the ideals behind the European Cup were less banausic than they have become.

Ten days before the game, fire gutted the central section of the Main Stand at Highfield Road. It looked as if a postponement might be necessary but temporary gantries were erected so that all season-ticket holders could be accommodated, and the game went ahead. The attendance of 47,111 was only ever bettered by that for the Wolves match.

There had been three wins on the trot in February, but the cloud descended with defeats by Everton and the eventual champions, Manchester City. The Thursday before the Manchester United

game was transfer deadline day; Ronnie Rees left for West Brom and Cantwell made two of his best signings, Cattlin and Hunt. Chris Cattlin was a young left-back from Huddersfield, the more experienced Ernie Hunt an inventive and pugnacious forward from Everton. 'Spider' and Ernie (real name Roger) soon made their mark.

City opened the scoring after 34 minutes when Ernie Machin volleyed past Alex Stepney from 30 yards out. Eight minutes after half-time, Ernie Hannigan, a skilful but erratic right-winger who was Cantwell's first signing, crossed for Setters to head a second. City held out despite United twice hitting the woodwork.

No one played a bigger part in defence than Chris Cattlin who had shackled George Best. Cattlin's father travelled from Lancashire for his son's debut. After the match, Matt Busby made a point of congratulating him on his son's performance. 'How are you getting home?' Busby asked. It was Cattlin Senior's proudest moment to sit beside the great man and be chauffeur-driven to the station, especially after his son had just played a major part in denting Manchester United's hopes of retaining their title.

The victory rocketed Coventry to the luxury of sixth from bottom, but there was another slide to come. Come Easter, the Sky Blues drew at Fulham, Brian Hill's goal countering Johnny Haynes' masterclass in accurate passing. During the game, George Cohen asked Ernie Hunt: 'How many fucking clubs do you play for?' The enquiry seemed pertinent as Hunt had already turned out at Craven Cottage that season for both Wolves and Everton. A brace of goals from Jimmy Greaves then did for City at White Hart Lane. The Sky Blues took only a point from their 2 penultimate games and were level with Sheffield United and Stoke on 32 points as they kicked off with Southampton.

The compactness of the Dell added to the desperate atmosphere of a dour and muddy game of few chances. Interest began to focus on a youth scurrying to-and-fro from the dugout. He was Coventry's youth team goalkeeper, David Icke. Icke's backstage calls brought little comfort to the City bench until the news that Chelsea had come from behind to win 2-1. Stoke, with a game in hand, made sure of safety with a draw at Leicester. At the end, a prostrate John Tudor needed to be revived to be told the good news. Maurice Setters had blobs of blood on his shirt from a cut eye, a warrior indeed. Southampton could only stand and watch as many of City's 7,000 supporters invaded the pitch.

In 1989, Ernie Hunt revealed in *The People* that he had acted on behalf of an independent party as the go-between in bribing four Southampton players, as he put it, 'not to bother'. The four players were allegedly on £1,000 a man to throw the game. 'We also had Chelsea players on a few bob that day to make sure that they did their best against Sheffield United,' said Hunt. Hunt also made claims about two other City matches, in 1969 and 1972, as well as a Leicester game in 1969.

Coventry City's confidence, unbridled a year before, had survived intact. The city was booming economically, League attendances at Highfield Road averaged nearly 35,000 and fans had cause to hope that their football club might one day really reach for the sky.

WOLVERHAMPTON WANDERERS v. COVENTRY CITY

15 April 1969
Molineux
Football League Division One
Wolverhampton Wanderers 1 Coventry City 1

	P	W	D	L	F	A	W	D	L	F	A	GA	P
15 Wolverhampton W.	39	7	9	4	25	21	3	5	11	14	30	0.7647	34
16 Sheffield Wednesday	38	7	7	5	25	24	3	6	10	13	25	0.7755	33
17 Stoke City	39	9	6	4	22	20	0	8	12	16	34	0.7037	32
18 Nottingham Forest	39	5	6	9	16	22	4	6	9	27	33	0.7818	30
19 Sunderland	39	9	6	5	26	18	0	6	13	12	46	0.5938	30
20 Coventry City	39	8	4	7	31	21	2	4	14	13	41	0.7097	28
21 Leicester City	36	6	7	5	23	22	1	4	13	9	37	0.5424	25
22 Queens Park Rangers	41	4	7	10	20	33	0	3	17	18	60	0.4086	18

Only those who were there to see this extraordinary game with their own eyes could possibly believe that one side could so outfight and outplay another team on its own ground and yet not win... So decisive were City, and so insipid were Wolves...

Derek Henderson, *Coventry Evening Telegraph*

There could hardly have been a Wolves follower among the 32,535 crowd at Molineux last night who would have offered anything but praise to Coventry if they had won this vital game as they fully deserved to do. It is not often in my twenty-one seasons with Wolves I have gone on record in terms like those, but there has to be a first time. The pity was it had to come on the last day of the home season when they [Wolves] might at least have tried to bow out with a show of pride and purpose.

Phil Morgan, *Wolverhampton Express and Star*

This was a surprising and somewhat unusual game. It was also a Coventry performance which Derek Henderson in the *Evening Telegraph* deemed the best away from home that City had produced in the First Division. The redoubtable Maurice Setters was at the heart of it. Dietmar Bruck added bite on his first appearance for nearly six months and Willie Carr was as effervescent as ever.

Thirty minutes had passed when the Sky Blues took the lead. Chris Cattlin's free-kick was headed on by Jeff Blockley to Ernie Hunt, who angled the ball in from almost on the byline. Coventry dictated the whole match. 'So decisive were City, and so insipid were Wolves,' observed Henderson. Yet, with 20 minutes left and entirely against the run of play, Wolves equalised. Setters was penalised for a challenge on Derek Dougan. A dallying David Wagstaffe was affecting the full gamut of preparation when Peter Knowles, younger brother of 'Nice One' Cyril and a Jehovah's Witness, suddenly pushed him aside. Knowles' accurate shot deflected past Bill Glazier. It turned out to be a rather costly goal for some. City continued to dominate but had to settle for a point.

'Apart from Parkes, who had to make one or two daring dives at the feet of eager forwards – and perhaps John Holsgrove – I do not recall a single Wolves player who emerged from this tawdry affair with any credit', commented Phil Morgan in the *Express and Star*, 'Wolves lacked the power to finish, as witness some incredible close-in misses, including two only yards from the line by Hugh Curran.'

Ian Gibson salutes the crowd at Highfield Road.

The Sky Blues completed the season with draws against Nottingham Forest and Liverpool. Leicester City, meantime, still had 5 games to play after losing the Cup Final to Manchester City. They needed 7 points (at 2 points for a win) to overhaul Coventry. A 1-0 home victory against Tottenham on the Tuesday after the final was followed by a 2-1 defeat at Ipswich on the Saturday. At Filbert Street the following Monday, they beat Sunderland 2-1. Two games to play, three points needed. There was a nine-day wait now for Everton. Everton, influenced particularly keenly by Alan Ball, played out of their skins as if it was they that were in Leicester's position, but a blunder by Gordon West and the sending-off of Colin Harvey enabled their hosts to grab a point. Three days later, 17 May, saw Matt Busby's last game in charge at Old Trafford. Leicester were a goal up after 3 minutes. Was this the torturous twist at the end of a long drawn-out story? Manchester United twice defied the woodwork but came back to win 3-2. It was a fitting and final testament to a great manager, not to mention a mighty relief for Coventry City.

City had started the season 2 games later than others because of the need to replace the main stand gutted by fire. The first 3 games were lost and for most of the season the League table resembled a skyscraper with broken lifts. Ian Gibson produced one of his most ingenious shows to prompt City's first win, when Hunt scored a hat-trick within the first 25 minutes against West Brom. There was some respite, but by the end of February Coventry had amassed a mere 14 points from 25 games.

Neil Martin missed the first 15 League games through injury. Meanwhile, City paid Liverpool £80,000 for Tony Hateley. When Bill Shankly opened negotiations for Hateley with Chelsea, he was told by Tommy Dochery: 'One hundred thousand wouldn't buy him.' Shankly retorted: 'I know, I'm one of the one hundred thousand.' Hateley had a good goalscoring record but his ball control was so poor it led to his Coventry team-mates nicknaming him Douglas, after Douglas Bader. There was no place for the player after Martin's return and it was no surprise when he was sold to Birmingham.

On 25 February, City crushed Q.P.R 5-0 in their first home match for ten weeks, won three on the trot, and in April repeated their victory against Manchester United of a year before. The most significant win though was against Leicester. Seven minutes from time, Leicester appeared to have won a penalty only for the referee to notice the linesman's flag raised for offside. Martin went on to score the only goal of the match.

After the game at Molineux, a police officer was injured when hooligans threw a brick through the driver's window of his panda car. 'The situation is getting serious and we are very perturbed,' said a police spokesman. A bottle was thrown through the window of a coach. The driver commented: 'What can be done about it? Nothing, as far as I can see, until some outside pressure is brought to bear.'

COVENTRY CITY v. MANCHESTER CITY

10 January 1970
Highfield Road
Football League Division One
Coventry City 3 Manchester City 0

This was the Manchester City of Summerbee, Bell and Lee – FA Cup holders, League Champions in 1968 and steered and coached by Joe Mercer and Malcolm Allison. They were one of the top attractions of the time. Coventry were no mean side either and for the first time were doing more than just making up the numbers. Joint Footballer of the Year Tony Book, that wise old bird with a face like an unmade bed, was missing from the visitors' line-up.

In the second match of the season, a first-half hat-trick by Willie Carr, playing as a makeshift striker, had destroyed West Brom at Highfield Road. Clearly, things were changing. More significant, in terms of confidence, were two away victories in the space of four days before the end of August. The Sky Blues had won only 3 away games in the whole of their first two seasons in the top flight.

City repeated the feat in October. They went to the Baseball Ground on a Wednesday night after winning at Highbury. The first of Brian Clough's great sides had taken little time to establish itself in the First Division. Derby conceded only 5 goals in their first 13 games and were unbeaten at home in 25 matches. Even Clough was moved to describe Coventry's 3-1 win as 'brilliant'.

In November, for the first time since 1958, George Curtis was dropped. Curtis, who is in every sense a monumental figure in the history of Coventry City, missed a chance against Manchester United from point-blank range. However, there was more to the end of his 534-game Coventry career than that, more even than the years that had caught up with the weeping George Mason. Noel Cantwell had signed a centre half from Dunfermline Athletic called Roy Barry.

Barry had attracted attention with his match-winning performance against W.B.A. in the European Cup-Winners Cup. At twenty-seven, he adjusted unusually quickly to the English League. Few people anticipated the immediate and stimulating effect a centre half could have in the days before players were expected to exercise a footballing brain in such a position. When goalkeepers could collect and distribute the ball with impunity, they traditionally hoofed it into an aerial mêlée where the prime function of the opposing centre half was to win the ball in the air. The consequent failure to recognise that a goalkeeper's punt often leads to a loss of possession was one of the reasons it took so long for British clubs to prevail in Europe.

Although he had been sent off several times in Scotland, once even for fighting with a teammate, Barry rarely fell foul of officials in England. Not only was he everything that was demanded of a conventional centre half but he also had the skill to be a superb organiser. He wore the players around him like puppets on his feet. City had a run of 8 wins in 9 League matches after Barry entered the side. The fifth on the trot was against Manchester City. All three goals came from headers. Neil Martin opened the scoring after 27 minutes from an Ernie Hunt cross and then, on either side of half-time, Ernie Machin laid on goals for John O'Rourke. O'Rourke, had been signed from Ipswich for £80,000 and was an England Under-23 international. It was an exciting signing. He looked to be just the right kind of foil for Martin.

City held the champions elect – Ball, Kendall, Harvey et al – to a goalless draw at Goodison Park. Only three other teams avoided defeat at Everton all season. Barry was the dominant figure but three weeks later, 12 minutes into the game at Hillsborough, he suffered a terrible broken leg in a

Right:
Highfield
Road 1970.

Far right:
Roy Barry
and Noel
Cantwell.

challenge on Tommy Craig for which he was booked. He was playing only his fourteenth match for the club. It would be the end of the following season again before he made even a single first-team appearance and sadly he would never quite sustain the same impact. It is an indication of the degree to which he had stirred the public imagination that a thousand people were at Ryton when he made his comeback in the 'A' team.

Despite the demoralising loss of Barry, City kept pegging away and lost only 2 of their remaining 10 games. An O'Rourke hat-trick helped beat Nottingham Forest at the City Ground and the Sky Blues clinched their place in Europe in the penultimate game with the only goal at Molineux. The goal was scored by Brian Joicey, who a year before had been playing amateur football for North Shields.

Bill Glazier was at his most agile in goal and Mick Coop and Chris Cattlin had outstanding seasons on either side of a defence, at the heart of which Jeff Blockley was now firmly established. Willie Carr, Dave Clements, Ian Gibson and Ernie Hunt provided fluent service for Martin and O'Rourke who scored 25 League goals between them.

City finished sixth, their highest ever position. They boasted an away record second only to Everton, winning 10 games.

'In what year did Coventry City last win the FA Cup?' the quiz-master asked a panel of Karl Marx, Lenin, Mao Tse-tung and Che Guevara. *Monty Python's Flying Circus* was flowering. By the end of 1969, the prospect of Coventry winning a major trophy had become no less plausible than the man on the moon.

COVENTRY CITY v. EVERTON

3 October 1970
Highfield Road
Football League Division One
Coventry City 3 Everton 1

On match day, as you walked round the corner to the main entrance of the ground, you might see the television vehicles and all the paraphernalia that go with an outside broadcast; you might glimpse a bank of screens in one of the vans, see a trail of cables a mile long, a ladder stretching into the sky with a cameraman perched on top like a sparrow on a giraffe's head. It has long since become an integral part of the scenery at League football grounds. There was a time when such a presence was a status symbol: the cameras were there, the world had come to admire you. If you blinked, there was more than just a report in the 'Pink' to describe what you had missed. In the vividness of colour still fresh to our screens, Ernie Hunt ambled urgently forward on *Match of the Day* to score one of the most extraordinary goals of the television age.

Before the start of the season, Bill Asprey, the Coventry coach, returned from a course at Lilleshall with a fresh idea for a free-kick. Ernie practised it a bit with Willie Carr. They tried it in a pre-season friendly at Blackpool but Hunt only succeeded in hitting the clock. For the moment, nothing more was said about it.

It had been an uneven start to the season. Five of the first ten matches were lost. Of 7 goals scored, 4 came at the Baseball Ground on one of City's great nights. The Sky Blues gave Derby a 2-goal start, Glazier saved a penalty, and Carr scored the winner 2 minutes from time. Four games followed without City scoring, but they were punctuated with 6 goals against Trakia Plovdiv in the European Fairs Cup.

Wilf Smith, who was signed from Sheffield Wednesday for £150,000 – a British record for a full-back, made his debut in the Derby match. Smith came with a big reputation and full international honours seemed inevitable. However, despite his undoubted ease on the ball, lack of pace counted against him. He was at his most effective for City in a defensive midfield role.

Everton wore their yellow change strip. Neil Martin put City ahead when he drew the ball wide in the box before scoring with an angled shot. John Hurst equalised. It was 1-1 at the break. 'Why didn't you try that free-kick?' Noel Cantwell asked Ernie. A conventional free-kick, from just outside the box, had clipped Brian Labone and gone wide. In the second half, Brian Alderson, making only his third full appearance, was unlucky not to score with a diagonal left-wing shot. As the ball came loose, Hunt needed to control the spin and scored from close-range. City won a free-kick, a chance to make it 3-1. This time, Ernie flipped his hand in a gesture to Carr as he hurried forward. Carr stood with his feet in a pincer around the ball with Hunt and Clements behind him. The alternative was for Hunt to poke the kick through Willie's legs and for Clements to run round and shoot, but Willie leapt into the air and, shaping himself like a seahorse, flicked the ball up vertically behind him. Hunt advanced four paces and struck the dropping ball with a dipping volley into the far corner of the net. Goal, what a goal! The sheer bravura of it, like a fiddler tearing off an arpeggio, was breathtaking. And the cameras were there to preserve it. It was 'Goal of the Season' – goal of most seasons for that matter.

It was a moment that caught the eye of Sean Day-Lewis, the *Sunday Telegraph* television critic:

The donkey-kick.

Television offered two memorable happenings over the weekend. In both there was a combination of superbly trained professional skills and outstanding inspiration, and both showed there are some things the medium can communicate better than anything else. One was the gripping performance of Donald Pleasance in Harold Pinter's *The Birthday Party*. The other was Coventry City's third goal against Everton.

The 'donkey-kick', as it affectionately became known, was later outlawed after a protest by pusillanimous Scottish referees. The ball, FIFA decided, did not travel its full circumference in the taking of the kcik. Carr and Hunt tried it a few more times that season but without success, although Hunt did hit the bar with it at Tottenham. Towards the end of his career, playing for Bristol City against West Bromwich, Ernie scored a spectacular variation, 'The Nutcracker'. This time, Hunt himself stood with his feet around the ball. Don Gillies then lifted the ball through Hunt's legs – hence 'The Nutcracker' – for Ernie to volley the ball into the net.

With his squat, square, bandy appearance, the chirpy and popular Hunt did not look much of an athlete but, as he swaggers into the mind's eye, he remains one of the most intuitive players to have represented the club.

No player, however, was more significant in enabling Coventry City to establish a personality at the top of English football than Willie Carr. The Glaswegian Carr arrived sprayed in freckles from school in Cambridge. Surely he was too small and delicate to make the grade. But Willie persevered with exceptional instinct and skill. Wheeling away with boundless enthusiasm, he transformed much around him that was ordinary into much that was outstanding.

After finishing sixth the previous season, 1970/71 was a bit of an anticlimax. City scored only 38 goals, their lowest total since 1919/20, but still finished tenth. The experienced Liverpool defender Geoff Strong had been bought to compensate for the extended absence of Roy Barry, and City continued to rely on the exceptional Bill Glazier and a resilient defence to make up for the lack of goals. The Sky Blues reached the League Cup quarter-finals but lost humiliatingly at Rochdale in the FA Cup. However, thanks to television, one goal, one moment from that season will live forever.

Bayern München v. Coventry City

20 October 1970
Stadion an der Grünwalder Strasse
European Fairs Cup Second Round First Leg
Bayern München 6 Coventry City 1

In the same year as Gordon Banks defied Pelé and the impossible, there were also some goalkeeping howlers. Peter Bonetti, Banks' understudy in the quarter-finals, returned from Mexico to be taunted from the terraces as 'The man who lost the World Cup!' When the Coventry players were invited to the cockpit on their flight home from Germany, Ernie Machin turned to Eric McManus and said: 'You'd better not take the controls, Eric, you might not hold on to them.'

It was a tribute to Eric McManus' temperament as well as his ability that after his pummelling in Munich the young 'keeper went on to enjoy such a long and dependable career. He made 396 League appearances, most of them for Notts County and Bradford City.

Bill Glazier had pulled a groin muscle on the Saturday. McManus, who was signed as a seventeen-year-old from Irish League Coleraine, had spent his first two years in the reserves, making only two First Division appearances. Suddenly, he found himself running out on a dreadful night to play against some of the most famous names in world football. Sepp Maier, Franz Beckenbauer and Gerd Müller had formed the spine of the West Germany World Cup side.

If McManus' performance was momentarily to attract notoriety, David Icke's subsequent career actually courted it. This was the closest that City's reserve goalkeeper on the night came to the first team. Arthritis finally forced him out of the game after a season with Hereford United. As a sports presenter, Icke then became one of the most ubiquitous faces on BBC Television. He later underwent a metamorphosis when a messianic vision galvanised him into confronting the world. Viewers looked on in lurid fascination when the warm smile turned into a scowl as he upbraided chat-show hosts. According to his publicity, he is: 'one of the most well-known and best fact-based conspiracy researchers on the globe today and because his information flies in the face of what we think about the world and some of its history he has been called the most controversial speaker in the world'. He is the author of several mighty tomes, including *Alice in Wonderland and the World Trade Center Disaster – Why the official story of 9/11 is a monumental lie.*

The rain in Munich was torrential. McManus made two saves at the start of the game and could not be held responsible for the opening goal after 4 minutes. Mick Coop slipped as he tackled Brenninger; Brenninger's cross was missed and Schneider seized on the opening to score. Six minutes later, City levelled as a result of their first serious attack. O'Rourke robbed Schwarzenbeck and Coop's cross found Ernie Hunt who headed past the flailing Maier. The elation of the small band of City supporters was short-lived. Bayern attacked down the left, Roth crossed, Brenninger passed and Schneider scored his second. McManus appeared to have left too much room by his near post and 4 minutes later he allowed Schwarzenbeck's speculative and dipping shot to skid past his right arm for a third goal. It was the decisive blow and, with only 19 minutes played, the Sky Blues went 4-1 down as a result of a cracking ground shot from Müller.

The match looked to be over as a contest. However, with a little luck, City might yet have got back into it. Coop's cross was met by Hunt's header and with Maier groping on the line the ball rapped against the post and slid away. Hunt then had a first-time effort hooked away by Schwarzenbeck. He had another prod at it before Maier got his arm in the way.

Coventry City, 1970. From left to right, back row: John O'Rourke, Bob Parker, Mick Coop, Trevor Gould, Ernie Hunt, Dietmar Bruck. Middle row: Dennis Mortimer, Brian Hill, Bill Glazier, Brian Joicey, Eric McManus, Billy Rafferty, Jeff Blockley. Front row: Ernie Machin, Chris Cattlin, Roy Barry, Noel Cantwell (manager), Neil Martin, David Clements, Willie Carr.

The confidence of the City players had been undermined by the absence of Glazier, even before they took to the field. Bayern had done more than enough to win comfortably but the Sky Blues showed guts as they mounted wave after wave of attacks. Some of the home supporters even booed their players for some slipshod work and for a time it looked as if City might at least emerge with their pride intact. McManus bravely got to a tremendous shot by Roth but in the last 15 minutes the sky finally fell in on both him and his team. A long-range shot from Roth found its way underneath his body for a fifth goal. In the dying moments, the youngster tamely turned a lob from the substitute Hoenef against the crossbar and Müller followed up to plant a header in the net. That was the end of it. McManus walked alone from the sodden field.

City had made the second leg an all-ticket match. Goals from Neil Martin and John O'Rourke restored some self-respect with City winning 2-1. Bayern Munich beat Sparta Rotterdam in the next round before losing in the quarter-finals to Liverpool.

A month earlier, forty intrepid supporters had flown out from Luton Airport, bath plugs in hand, to penetrate one of the most austere corners of the Iron Curtain. The rest of us tuned in anxiously to the sports news on the radio: Trakia Plovdiv 1, Coventry City 4. The report said that O'Rourke had scored a hat-trick with the other goal coming from Martin. Gypsy fiddlers swooped and swooned at the reception as the Sky Blues entourage celebrated a distinguished European debut. A fortnight later, Brian Joicey and Jeff Blockley completed the job to give City a 6-1 aggregate victory.

It was Coventry's only European campaign. What might have been but for Roger Osborne's Cup Final winner for Ipswich against Arsenal in 1978, or for the ban affecting English clubs in 1987?

ARSENAL v. COVENTRY CITY

4 November 1972
Highbury
Football League Division One
Arsenal 0 Coventry City 2

Somewhere in the BBC archives, there may still be a news clip of it. Before cameras came to record every move in every match, you dared not turn away for fear of missing an unrepeatable moment. One such moment was Tommy Hutchison's goal at Highbury.

Much had changed. In March, Noel Cantwell was sacked – Derrick Robins preferring to inform him by letter. Cantwell later commented that 'Jimmy Hill's ghost followed me around the dressing room.' He rescued the Sky Blue dream when it was in danger of being shattered and took the club into Europe. However, attendances were slipping and his teams bore an increasingly inflexible, defensive and one-paced look.

At the beginning of the previous season, Cantwell appointed new backroom staff. The former England goalkeeper, Tony Waiters, became first-team coach and Ian St John joined the club as player/assistant manager. The greatest need was for a goalscorer. Chris Chilton, who had scored an abundance of goals during a long career at Hull City, only had a few left in his locker. His old club knocked City out of the Cup.

Bob Dennison, the chief scout and former Northampton and Middlesbrough manager, took over from Cantwell in a caretaker capacity. By the beginning of April, City had gone 11 league games without a win and were sliding into trouble. Then came Everton. Even the normally dependable Johnny Morrissey was having an off-day as City won 4-1. Relegation was comfortably avoided but the public waited expectantly for a new manager and a new dynamic.

Dennison had been Brian Clough's manager at Middlesbrough. 'Dennison taught me by accident, through incompetence. I learned what not to do,' Clough wrote. Clearly, not everyone had shared Clough's assessment of him as 'hopeless'.

It was Clough himself who came so close to becoming the new Coventry manager. Derrick Robins had received permission from the Derby chairman, Sam Longson, to talk to him. 'His offer was staggering,' Clough wrote. 'No one manager would have been on more than me had I gone. The incentives were tremendous – the contract, with its salary and bonuses, unbelievable.' The deal also involved Peter Taylor and trainer Jimmy Gordon. With Derby on their way to the title, the only thing that could not be agreed on was the timing. Robins wanted them to join the club straight away and subsequently withdrew his offer. 'Had Mr Robins known that twenty-four hours earlier we had resigned, I am certain that he would have welcomed us all,' wrote Clough.

One of the many applicants for the post was Joe Mercer. In June, Coventry sought to replicate the success of Mercer's partnership with Malcolm Allison at Manchester City by offering the genial grandee the post of general manager. Gordon Milne, the former Liverpool and England wing half, who had been managing non-league Wigan and the England Youth team, became team manager.

In October, Coventry made two major signings: Colin Stein, the Glasgow Rangers and Scotland centre forward, and Milne's former team-mate at Blackpool, Tommy Hutchison. Stein was one of the very biggest names in Scottish football, a strong, mobile player with good control and plenty of goals. Hutchison was one of a handful of outrageously gifted British players who led us to look at that era of domestic football through rose-tinted spectacles. He defied the normal squatness of Scottish wingers. Hutch was tall with legs up to his elbows. High cheek-bones were chiselled into

Tommy Hutchison.

his face. He could have recoiled out of a spaghetti western – all that was missing was the hat. He would nibble at, then bamboozle his opponent. With a swish of the hips, he'd lasso him in a whirlwind of legs and be off, leaving the crowd gasping and smiling in his wake.

Thus it was at Highbury. Hutchison took a throw-in just inside the Arsenal half. Alan Ball surrendered possession and there was Hutch on the left wing ready to pick things up. Hutchison was right-footed but carried the ball with his left. Ball's tackle almost toppled him but Rice's was disdained in one extended stride. By now, Hutch had crossed the halfway line. He was bearing down on the Clock End. McLintock was left sprawling by a characteristic swerve. Geoff Barnett came off his line. Hutch cut inside and took the ball to the near post. He shot from a narrow angle with Arsenal players desperately running back. It was not a shot that shouted – it didn't need to be. Tommy Hutchison had torn Arsenal to shreds in one fell swoop.

Nick Hornby, in *Fever Pitch*, described Coventry fans as: 'cavorting around on the Clock End like dolphins.' He went on: 'Then came the fierce, unanimous and heartfelt chant from the Arsenal fans: "You're going to get your fucking heads kicked in."'

The goal came 15 minutes from the end of the game. Jeff Blockley, in his last match for Coventry a few weeks before, had scored an own goal with a gorgeous lob over Bill Glazier's head. Only days after signing for Arsenal, he won his single England cap. Facing his former club, Blockley was given a torrid time by Stein whose right-wing cross, headed in by Alderson, had already helped to give City the lead after 10 minutes.

Brian Alderson had been converted into a lethal foil for Stein. He joined Coventry from a Scottish junior club, Lochie Harp, as a fast, direct winger. In the swing of his arms, he resembled a speeded up film of someone wading into water. He could also unleash a shot almost as powerfully as Peter Lorimer.

The Sky Blues were in the middle of an 8-match unbeaten run which ended on a return visit to Ipswich. Ten days before, City had been leading at Portman Road with a goal from Stein when the floodlights failed.

Hutchison's wonderful goal is one of the great treasures of City's heritage. It also defined a fresh panache about the club and its football.

MIDDLESBROUGH V. COVENTRY CITY

19 October 1974
Ayresome Park
Football League Division One
Middlesbrough 4 Coventry City 4

The miners voted for a national strike. In February, when Edward Heath went to the country over the issue of who runs Britain, his government unexpectedly fell. As a result of the international oil crisis, a three-day week in factories and offices was imposed and a 50mph speed limit on all roads.

On Sunday 27 January 1974, Highfield Road attracted what was to be its last crowd of over 40,000, for the visit of Derby in the FA Cup. Floodlighting was banned during the power crisis and the game kicked-off at two o'clock. Derrick Robins wrote an editorial in the programme:

> Some four years ago I fought at the annual general meeting of the Football League for permission for professional clubs to play football on whatever day suited them and their supporters best, and whilst I felt I carried the bulk of the thousand people in the room I was defeated on the voting... Sunday football need not in any way be detrimental to the church, its principles and the many people who are so closely involved with it. Indeed, providing the times do not clash, Sunday football could go a long way to making the Sabbath a very happy day indeed.

The goalless draw was a disappointment but City won the replay 1-0. They went out agonisingly in a fifth round replay at Q.P.R., Stan Bowles scoring with almost the last kick of an exhilarating match. The Sky Blues got even closer to Wembley in the League Cup. They were 2-1 ahead in a replay at Maine Road, with a semi-final against Plymouth Argyle in prospect, only for Manchester City to score three times in the last 12 minutes.

In 1972/73, Coventry reached the quarter-finals of the FA Cup but a 2-0 defeat at Molineux presaged a decline which culminated in City losing their last 7 League games. There was a slight improvement in League form in 1973/74 with the Sky Blues finishing sixteenth; they had been second at the end of September. It was a period which saw the establishment of more members of the extraordinary class of 1970: Holmes, Dugdale, Cartwright, Green and McGuire. Bobby Parker and Dennis Mortimer had already made their mark, although Parker's confidence may have been broken by his bad error in the Wolves Cup-tie. There were also new faces: John Craven – an experienced presence in central defence or midfield and also as captain, David Cross – a tall and reliable striker, even if not in the class of Martin or Stein, and Larry Lloyd. Lloyd, an England international, arrived from Anfield for a Coventry record of £240,000. Sadly, he is recalled now at Highfield Road as much for a freakish goal he scored from the halfway line in a Cup-tie against Norwich as for any consistency in his defensive displays. More pertinently, the financial embarrassment engendered by his signing threatened the economic stability of the club. City hoped they were going to raise most of the money for Lloyd by selling Jimmy Holmes and Mick McGuire to Tottenham. The deal fell through when Bill Nicholson was sacked, leaving Coventry substantially in the red. City were eventually grateful to accept a £60,000 offer for Lloyd from Second Division Nottingham Forest. At Forest, he became the fulcrum Gordon Milne envisaged at Coventry.

One of the most poignant episodes of the era surrounded the departure of Carr. It was not just that Coventry had agreed to sell him to their rivals Wolves. There was something slightly shocking about the very idea of Willie Carr leaving Coventry City. A talented team had been taking shape

Right: Dennis Mortimer.

Far right: Larry Lloyd and Joe Mercer.

around him and he had become more than an excuse for optimism, he was the symbol of it. Worse still, he then failed his medical on account of a knee injury. A year later, Wolves signed him for a third of the £240,000 the two clubs had originally agreed. Happily, he was to enjoy the many further years at the top that his talent merited.

The 1974/75 season got off to a wretched start but City were beginning to find their feet by the time they went to Ayresome Park. Jack Charlton was the manager at Middlesbrough and had built his team around a defence as uncompromising as it sounded: Platt, Craggs, Spraggon, Boam, Maddren. Even a player of the finesse of Graeme Souness contributed to the hard edge but this was an afternoon when excitement prevailed. The Sky Blues opened the scoring against the run of play, Colin Stein collecting a long pass from Lloyd. Stein, who had already taken a knock, was immediately replaced by Brian Alderson. Souness then put Middlesbrough ahead with two goals, the first from 25 yards and the second ricocheting off Graham Oakey. City found themselves 2 down shortly after half-time when David Mills scored with a close-range effort. This did not signal any capitulation though and Cross pulled a goal back with a header after 56 minutes. Eight minutes later, City were back on terms with another memorable goal – this time a blistering shot from Jimmy Holmes. Bill Glazier's magnificent career at Coventry was drawing to a close and his successor, Neil Ramsbottom, was in goal. Ramsbottom made a fine save from John Hickton but Alan Foggon was there to make it 4-3. The afternoon was not over. With 3 minutes left, Holmes unleashed another volley to tie the parcel up to everyone's satisfaction.

In 1974, in the wake of Alf Ramsey's dismissal, City's general-manager Joe Mercer also took on the caretaker managership of England. In April 1975, it was announced that Derrick Robins was retiring to South Africa. The industrial troubleshooter Sir Jack Scamp was shortly to assume the chairmanship from Robins' son, Peter. Derrick Robins had already left the board and become club president. It is a tribute to how far he had brought the club that when he prefaced his comments in the club's official brochure in 1970 with the announcement: 'We are going to become the Real Madrid of England,' no one saw any reason to titter. As a benefactor and man of vision, he is one of the most important figures in the history of the club and his partnership with Jimmy Hill was pivotal to the modern development of Coventry City. Coincidentally, as Derrick Robins departed, Jimmy Hill returned to the club as managing director.

COVENTRY CITY v. BRISTOL CITY

19 May 1977
Highfield Road
Football League Division One
Coventry City 2 Bristol City 2

	P	W	D	L	F	A	W	D	L	F	A	GD	P
18 Sunderland	41	9	5	7	29	16	2	7	11	17	36	-6	34
19 Bristol City	41	8	7	6	25	19	3	5	12	11	27	-10	34
20 Coventry City	41	7	8	5	32	24	3	6	12	14	33	-11	34
21 Stoke City	42	9	8	4	21	16	1	6	14	7	35	-23	34
22 Tottenham Hotspur	42	9	7	5	26	20	3	2	16	22	52	-24	33

The final few minutes of this match were probably the most bizarre that any of those present would ever witness. A score-flash on the gigantic scoreboard at the back of the Spion Kop said it all: Everton 2 Sunderland 0.

With their First Division survival in the balance, the two Citys kicked-off at 7.30 p.m. – except that they didn't kick-off at 7.30 p.m. There had been severe traffic congestion and many of the 36,903 crowd were still outside the ground. 'In his wisdom, the referee delayed the kick-off fractionally, not more than 5 minutes, so the game started late,' Jimmy Hill wrote in his autobiography.

At the start of the season, supporters looked forward to seeing City build on their steady League form of the previous two years. The 1975/76 season had finished as it began, with a David Cross hat-trick. It also saw the signing of Bryan King, an experienced and highly regarded goalkeeper from Millwall, who never lived up to expectations and whose career was soon ended by injury. That opened the door for the brilliant young Scotsman, Jim Blyth. Belief in the club's ambition had been shaken by the sale, to Aston Villa, of Dennis Mortimer. Mortimer was undoubtedly one of the most gifted players the club ever produced, a scouser with a sixties shock of dark hair, gliding suavely forward from midfield and bobbing like a ten-pin perfectly poised. He skippered Villa's League Championship and European Cup-winning teams, and was unlucky never to win a full England cap.

On 27 August 1976, City unveiled three new signings who were to have a profound effect on the team: Bobby McDonald, Terry Yorath and a young striker from Dumbarton, Ian Wallace. The new-found confidence, however, began to melt. Bad weather prevented City from playing a single home League match between 22 January and 2 April. A promising team was slipping inexorably into trouble. It was time for Gordon Milne to receive the dreaded vote of confidence.

Stoke and Tottenham were already relegated. Sunderland, Bristol City and Coventry were level on points going into their final matches. Goal difference, that arithmetical black cap, threatened to be decisive.

Such considerations were superfluous with the Sky Blues in front. Tommy Hutchison opened the scoring after 15 minutes when goalkeeper John Shaw palmed a cross into his path. Coventry were in control, despite some occasional flutters. Bobby McDonald cleared off his line and Les Sealey saved a Trevor Tainton shot from just outside the area. Another shot then squeezed through Sealey's legs, narrowly missing a post.

Hutchison began to tease and turn it on. After 52 minutes, he scored a second goal, his shot going in off the bar after Barry Powell hit a post.

Alan Dicks and Gordon Milne.

The relief was short-lived. Within a minute, Gerry Gow scored with a low shot after some neat play with Don Gillies. The confidence of the Coventry players was draining as tangibly as their opponents' adrenaline was beginning to pump. An equaliser suddenly became more likely. And sure enough, with 11 minutes remaining, it came. Gillies overlapped and threaded a shot in at the near post. Bristol City needed only to hang on; the Sky Blues had to score to be sure of safety. Desperation crept in. We were suddenly aware of the chill in the evening air.

City fans visiting Goodison Park a fortnight earlier could read notices requesting them to 'Please Refrain From Throwing Missiles.' All of a sudden, the advice coming from Goodison was of a rather different nature. Like a swarm of bees, it was stirring a minor commotion. Heads turned, not towards an outbreak of fisticuffs in the crowd but towards the directors' box. The excitement was in a flick of the switch and bore no relation to what was happening on the pitch. It was the news that Sunderland had lost. The equaliser that would have sent us down never came; indeed Everton had scored a second through Bob Latchford. On the field, the players immediately grasped the implication. If the score at Highfield Road remained at 2-2, Sunderland – and not Coventry or Bristol City – would be relegated. As a match, the game in front of us drained as suddenly as a bath. It needed only the final, formal blast of the referee's whistle to signal the end of term. The two teams ground to a halt as the players aimlessly passed the ball around among themselves. The score from Goodison shone intensely from the scoreboard in the fading light. The referee did not compound the embarrassment by playing any injury time. Those 5 minutes had seemed interminable.

Alan Dicks, the Bristol City manager who was Jimmy Hill's assistant at Highfield Road in the 1960s, poured the champagne for Gordon Milne. Everyone was happy, except for Sunderland. The late kick-off would come back to haunt them twenty years later. Undoubtedly, it proved felicitous for Coventry but as Jimmy Hill wrote: 'The referee confirmed that it was solely his decision to delay the kick-off and the club was not concerned in any way.' Alan Hardaker, the Football League secretary, took more convincing. He wrote a letter of reprimand to the club who then took legal advice. 'We want this decision rescinded and the stain removed from Coventry's name', wrote the board. The League backed down.

COVENTRY CITY v. NORWICH CITY

27 December 1977
Highfield Road
Football League Division One
Coventry City 5 Norwich City 4

A few months after a fretful fling with relegation and with only a tweaking of the team, Coventry City were beginning to overwhelm opponents and provide a consistent level of entertainment unfamiliar in the decade since promotion.

The experienced Aston Villa right-winger Ray Graydon, who only stayed until March, was the one newcomer. He and Tommy Hutchison provided the crosses for Mick Ferguson and Ian Wallace in an all-out 4-2-4 formation. Gordon Milne was lucky to have two such tireless players in midfield as Terry Yorath and Barry Powell. Yorath's captaincy, besides his tackling and distribution, proved an unusually decisive dynamic. Powell had the purposefulness, if not quite the guile, of a Carr or a Strachan. Jim Holton, the former Scotland centre half who had arrived in March, was an influential figure in a defence sometimes left exposed by the team's devil-may-care attack. Mick Coop moved into the middle next to Holton with Graham Oakey and Bobby McDonald on either side. McDonald, an accomplished full-back, made 160 consecutive League appearances for the club. Oakey, a slightly built but quick and skilful player much beloved by fans for his tremendous enthusiasm, suffered a Boxing Day injury at Villa Park that finished his career.

Ferguson and Wallace rolled back the years and reminded older fans of Bourton and Lauderdale plundering goals in the days of 'The Old Five'. They scored 38 goals between them out of a total of 75, City's highest since 1963/64. The upright Ferguson was the target man as Wallace, with his fluffy mop of ginger hair, swept up. However, such a caricature does scant justice to the versatility of the two players.

City had gone five games without a win, including a 6-0 defeat at Everton. With Holton and Coop injured, the Sky Blues were forced to play Yorath and Beck in defence with Ray Gooding coming into midfield for his first game of the season. Powell opened the scoring with a penalty – it was City's 500th First Division goal. Wallace then made it 2-0 with an extraordinary effort. The ball reached him at head height with his back to goal near the penalty spot. He was hemmed in by defenders but produced an acrobatic leap and an overhead bicycle kick that rocketed the ball into the net. Norwich fought back and scored three goals – a John Ryan penalty and 2 from Kevin Reeves, in the 13 minutes before half-time. An earlier effort from Martin Peters was disallowed for offside.

Incredibly, the second half was even more eventful than the first. Gooding lashed the ball home from the edge of the area for his first City goal and then, 10 minutes later, McDonald restored the lead with a curling shot past goalkeeper Kevin Keelan. The Sky Blues had 2 more goals disallowed. Peters levelled the scores at 4-4 and then hit a post with a free-kick. With 9 minutes to go, Graydon headed over Keelan to make it 5-4 but even then the excitement was not over.

Norwich were awarded a penalty – the third of the match. There were 90 seconds to go. Ryan stepped up again and shot to his left. Jim Blyth plunged to make a brilliant match-winning save.

5-4 it was. 'Those who were here today were privileged,' said Norwich manager John Bond. Gordon Milne missed the game. He was away on a scouting mission.

It was an exceptional season. Another memorable match was the one against Manchester City on 4 October. Manchester City came to Highfield Road as unbeaten League leaders and had

Ian Wallace and Mick Ferguson.

conceded only 4 goals in 8 games. They were ahead after only 4 minutes when Dennis Tueart scored from Joe Royle's headed pass. The Sky Blues equalised on the half hour when, against the run of play, John Beck pulled the ball back for Ferguson to score. Just before half-time, Peter Barnes restored the visitors' lead from a long pass by Kenny Clements. In the second half, the Sky Blues attacked incessantly but without success until, in the 73rd minute, Powell set Oakey free on the right. Oakey's pass was flicked on by Beck for Ferguson to lob Joe Corrigan and make it 2-2. Six minutes later, Ferguson scaled the defence to head the ball down for Wallace to score. In the final minute, Ferguson chested Hutchison's left-wing cross before placing the ball wide of Corrigan to complete his hat-trick and a 4-2 victory.

Later in the month, at Molineux, Ferguson scored another hat-trick. A third, against Birmingham with 13 games left to play, were his last goals of the season. He missed 9 games through injury and City went on to win only 1 of their last 8 matches. The Sky Blues finished seventh, Ipswich's unexpected victory in the Cup Final denying them a place in Europe.

There were goals galore at Highfield Road. City also hit 4 against Q.P.R., Birmingham and Wolves. There was a 3-0 win against Manchester United and a 5-1 thrashing of Chelsea, besides victory over the eventual champions, Liverpool. It was one of the most satisfying and exciting seasons in the club's history.

COVENTRY CITY v. CRYSTAL PALACE

6 September 1980
Highfield Road
Football League Division One
Coventry City 3 Crystal Palace 1

Should someone have shot the ref! As mistakes go, Mr Webb's was as bad as they get.

Refereeing errors even themselves out over a season, or so we are told. By the law of averages, our opponents are not alone in benefiting from controversial decisions. And however intimidating we perceive the great citadels of the game to be to the fair-mindedness of the arbitrator in the middle, you will not find an Arsenal or Manchester United fan who feels any differently towards him than a Coventry or Crystal Palace one.

Football has always been a game of goodies and baddies, of us and them, the subjective and the objective. Scepticism about the ref is all part of it. Wouldn't it be boring if we could all agree that referees were honest, let alone able? What else would we talk about?

Yet, referee-bashing has become an insidious poison, which drip-feeds throughout the game and leads to a regular abuse and even assault of officials, on pitches where there may be nothing more at stake than parental pride or personal bullishness. Despite the tedious level of dissent, football's guardians – mindful of sponsors and the courts – are often reluctant to take a stand. Meantime, listen to the duplicitous drivel of many a manager which goes unchallenged at the end of a game.

Consider too the cosy mantra we love to parrot about inconsistency. And if a player gets booked for giving the ref a mouthful over a duff decision, who do we blame when it leads to suspension? We scream at officials over offside from behind the goal without even noticing when fans sitting side-on are unmoved. Television pundits sometimes pontificate without the support of a camera in line with the action.

Most television analysis relates in some way to refereeing decisions. Why is it therefore that television never allows us to hear the views of anyone who has had any experience of being a referee? Must we always depend on the outlook of former players, current ones too? Jimmy Hill, when he first presented *Match of the Day*, analysed certain incidents through the eyes of the referee, explaining the law and demonstrating that a ref is not a 'cheat' because he makes a wrong decision. How many other people in the game could be sufficiently confident of their knowledge to run the line in a League match, as Hill once did in an emergency at Highbury?

The paying public have become pawns in a wider game. Football serves to sell satellite dishes and to bloat the newspapers, newspapers that were once filled with matters of real life and death. Nowadays, what counts is contentiousness.

The players do not make it easy, whether it be Ian Wright following through on Steve Ogrizovic's head or the saintly young Michael Owen pulling a 'fly-in-the-eye' stunt on David Burrows. Coventry City players, of course, never do such things.

Sometimes though, the balance of justice is so unfair that it is like putting a large bag of cement on the kitchen scales. On 20 May 1963, the ball-boy in his coracle on the river Severn outside Gay Meadow awaited the last stray shots of that freezing winter. Inside the ground, Shrewsbury Town were playing Coventry City. With the scores at 1-1 and with only 15 minutes left to play, a shot from John Gregson, the Shrewsbury outside right, appeared to enter the Coventry goal through a hole in the side netting. The referee, Mr Leslie Tirebuck, gave a goal. Jimmy Hill said: 'There is no doubt about it. The ball went outside the post. You only had to see the reaction of the players –

'The decisions of the referee regarding facts connected with play are final'.

including the "scorer" – to know that.' George Curtis and Ronnie Farmer were booked for dissent. Farmer said afterwards: 'The Shrewsbury players told us they admitted it went through the hole – including Gregson.' The most likely explanation is that the linesman did not adequately check the nets before kick-off. Coventry had to wait seventeen years to balance the scales of this injustice.

Clive Allen, Britain's first million-pound teenager, sparked the Palace game into life with an opportunist goal just after half-time, when he punished Paul Dyson and David Jones for their defensive errors. However, within 6 minutes Coventry were ahead. Both goals were scored by City's new signing, Gerry Daly. And then it happened.

The *Match of the Day* recording showed that a shot from Clive Allen struck the stanchion in the back top corner of the net and flew back into play at lightning pace. Referee Derek Webb, after consulting both linesmen, disallowed the goal, clearly believing the ball had hit the angle of the bar and post. The Palace players were incandescent with rage. Their manager, a certain Mr Venables, had this to say: 'It was a disgrace. I feel we would have had something out of the match if that goal had counted. But the referee's decision demoralised us. Perhaps he wanted us to hit a particular part of the net before he gave a goal.' Gordon Milne offered sympathy: 'I feel sorry for Terry and his team because I had no doubt it was a goal. But to be fair to the referee, if he thought the ball had come back off the woodwork then he could not give a goal. He can only give what he sees.'

Neville Foulger's comments in the *Coventry Evening Telegraph* were prescient:

> Suggestions that referees should be allowed to see the television playback of incidents such as this before making a decision are ludicrous – unless television cameras are to be at every match in the country... But it should be said that, even in the Press Box, opinion was divided... had the television cameras not been at the match, we would still be arguing... basing a decision on opinion rather than hard evidence by slow-motion film.

The Sky Blues, for whom yet another teenager, Peter Bodak, was making his debut, went on to score a third goal through Andy Blair.

Let us hope that no one could ever come to ponder the proposal in the opening sentence.

COVENTRY CITY v. WEST HAM UNITED

27 January 1981
Highfield Road
Football League Cup Semi-Final First Leg
Coventry City 3 West Ham United 2

The Sky Blues' first major cup semi-final was the high spot of the declining period of Gordon Milne's managership. It also revived the excitement that had dissipated all too quickly after the 1977/78 season.

Before the start of the 1978/79 campaign, Milne made two significant signings: Gary Gillespie and Steve Hunt. At seventeen, Gillespie had been captaining Falkirk in addition to being a bank clerk. Like a sentry, he held his torso as straight as a stick insect. He was rarely ruffled and became one of the outstanding City players of the period. Hunt had been released by Aston Villa before finding his feet with New York Cosmos. He was an effective addition to the left side of City's midfield and went on to win two England caps after his five-and-a-half years at Coventry.

In January 1979, Coventry hit the headlines when they became the first British club to offer a £1,000,000 transfer fee; it was quite a turnaround for a club so recently in the financial doldrums. The player involved was England international Trevor Francis. Francis, however, opted to join Nottingham Forest.

Earlier that season, the Sky Blues came from behind to defeat Derby with three goals in the last 11 minutes and, at the end of March, beat Manchester United 4-3 in a match also made memorable by the performance of Garry Thompson. A potentially brilliant career was interrupted for almost a year when Thompson suffered a badly broken leg a fortnight later. City finished tenth in the table.

Two defenders, Gary Collier and David Jones, were signed in the summer of 1979 for a total of £575,000. Collier was the first player to move clubs through freedom of contract, Jones later managed Southampton and Wolves. The two expensive acquisitions only started 11 matches between them.

City slipped to fifteenth and Cup defeat at Third Division Blackburn. Neither Mick Ferguson, who scored all 4 City goals in the home game against high-flying Ipswich, nor Jim Holton, played again after New Year's Day, on account of injuries.

Jimmy Hill succeeded the retiring Phil Mead as chairman in the close season of 1980. Hill's first major decision was to sell Ian Wallace to Nottingham Forest for £1,250,000. The money helped finance the Sky Blue Connexion, a sports and social complex opened by the Duke of Edinburgh at the Ryton training ground on the outskirts of the city. The ghost of the Wallace sale haunted supporters for years to come. The Connexion proved to be a white elephant and was eventually sold for less than half what it cost. It was then leased back to the club. Coventry City broke new ground by signing a sponsorship deal with the Talbot car group but the FA refused to sanction a change of name to Club Coventry Talbot.

Coventry were developing some exceptional young players. Besides Gillespie, there were Paul Dyson and Danny Thomas in defence, Andy Blair in midfield, winger Peter Bodak, and Garry Thompson and Mark Hateley up front, giving the side an average age of under twenty-one. The 'old hands' were Les Sealey, 'Harry' Roberts – who had taken over from Bobby McDonald at left-back, Steve Hunt and Gerry Daly. Daly, the oldest at twenty-six, had been signed from Derby for £300,000 and was the most skilful playmaker City possessed over the next few years.

Above left: The Duke of Edinburgh opens the Sky Blue Connexion, November 1980.

Above right: From left to right, back row: Danny Thomas, Brian Roberts, Andy Blair. Front row: Peter Bodak, Paul Dyson, Gary Gillespie, Garry Thompson, Les Sealey, Steve Hunt, Mark Hateley, Gerry Daly.

The League Cup run had started with 1-0 victories in both legs against Manchester United. Tommy Hutchison returned from a summer playing in America and scored the winner in an outstanding personal performance at Brighton. Few expected when he was sold to Manchester City shortly afterwards that, at the age of thirty-three, some of his best football lay ahead of him. City reached the quarter-finals by beating Cambridge in an away replay; Sealey saved a penalty and Hunt volleyed a superb winner. After a 2-2 draw at Watford, the Sky Blues crushed the Hornets 5-0 in a memorable replay. Liverpool, Manchester City and West Ham also reached the semi-finals. West Ham were in the Second Division and consequently there was a real buzz that this might be City's year.

Whatever the expectations, the greater experience of Billy Bonds, Trevor Brooking and ex-City striker David Cross soon had the Sky Blues reeling. The Hammers helped themselves to a seemingly unassailable lead after 35 minutes. A mistake by Sealey presented a soft header to Bonds and, 8 minutes later, Thompson was inconsolable after scoring an own-goal. Hunt's clenched fist to the West End was a rallying call. Thompson made amends 18 minutes from time when he pulled a goal back, Phil Parkes having repelled everything in the Hammers' goal. The youthful exuberance of the Coventry team took fire. Five minutes later, City were on level terms. Daly scored after Parkes parried a fierce shot from Thomas. West Ham had a goal disallowed for offside 5 minutes from time but there was one more twist to come. With almost the last kick of the game, Thompson flat-footed Alvin Martin and let rip with the winner into the left-hand corner.

This thrilling game captivated City fans more than any other of its era. Thompson's character and determination had made the difference. The effort and ability of so much home-grown talent had endeared itself to people's hearts.

A fortnight later at Upton Park, City made defensive errors and lost the second leg 2-0. Jimmy Neighbour scored the decider in the last minute to add to Paul Goddard's goal earlier in the second half. City's season fell away. Seven defeats in 8 league games led to a brush with relegation. In the close season, Dave Sexton took over from Gordon Milne who became general manager. West Ham lost the final to Liverpool after a replay, but won the Second Division Championship.

SOUTHAMPTON v. COVENTRY CITY

4 May 1982
The Dell
Football League Division One
Southampton 5 Coventry City 5

Football people may not keep track of sequences like a gambler does at the roulette wheel, but for years there was an obstinate consistency about the results of Southampton v. Coventry matches. Just as Southampton went 26 games between 1950 and 1987 without winning at Highfield Road, so Coventry went 22 games between 1939 and 1979 without winning at the Dell. No one though would have bet on the scoreline of this encounter.

League records show that when fans made their way through the turnstiles that evening, there were over fifty other more likely permutations of result that they could expect to witness. It was as unlikely to be a 5-5 draw as it was for the visitors to win 7-1 or the hosts to win 9-0 or 9-1 – or 8-2 for that matter. This was the twenty-seventh instance of a 5-5 draw in a League game and the first since Chelsea v. West Ham in 1966/67. When Sheffield Wednesday drew 5-5 at home to Everton in 1904/05, they had been 5 down at half-time. There have been only two higher scoring draws, both 6-6. As customers took their places at the Dell, there were more important considerations at stake in the Falkland Islands: *HMS Sheffield* was sunk that night.

Dave Sexton was the new man in charge at Coventry. His reserved manner was belied by a serrated profile which could have been moulded by boxing. Indeed, his father Archie Sexton had been a boxer and fought Jock McAulay for the British middleweight title in 1933. Sexton came as one of the most respected coaches in the game. He was a successful former manager of Chelsea and – so close to the Busby years – not a successful enough manager of Manchester United. He joined Coventry in May 1981, a month after his dismissal from Old Trafford.

The eminence of the new manager was an encouragement to City supporters but Sexton himself was to discover that the board's agenda was complicated by other concerns. The season kicked off at Highfield Road with a 2-1 win against – of all clubs – Manchester United, for whom Ron Atkinson was the new manager. Publicity, however, was focused on the all-seater arrangement at Highfield Road which had reduced the capacity to 20,500.

In his autobiography, Jimmy Hill wrote: 'Never mind the 51,500 who witnessed the match against Wolverhampton... the average crowds since those years varied between thirteen and seventeen thousand'. He should have said between nineteen and thirty-five thousand. Coventry were among the eleven best supported teams in the country during their first three seasons in Division One. Despite a steep decline, the average of 16,904 in 1980/81 was unprecedentedly low and the only time it had dropped under 19,000. As recently as 1978/79 it was 22,638. It appeared therefore that a large number of people could potentially be denied the opportunity to support their local football team. Aberdeen was the only other club in Britain to have adopted a seats-only policy. It had reduced the capacity at Pittodrie to 24,000, an ample limit even at that time of great Aberdeen success. As autumn dampened, City fans sitting exposed on the Spion Kop end were to cast an increasingly rueful eye at the directors' box. Tickets were expensive and had to be bought at least forty-eight hours before the game. Not surprisingly, the average dropped to 13,100 by the end of the season and to 10,552 in 1982/83. Coventry's investment in football in America had been a disaster and resulted in the loss of hundreds of thousands of pounds. The involvement of Talbot as Coventry City sponsor was seen by many as a threat to the club's identity rather than of significant mutual benefit.

Above left: 'It's been like this throughout every match since the deal with Talbot.'

Above right: Danny Thomas, Coventry City and England.

Against this background, Sexton nonetheless managed to shape his young charges. Steve Jacobs had replaced Andy Blair, who was sold to Aston Villa, and other youngsters such as Steve Whitton and Ian Butterworth were introduced. A 5-1 thumping by Notts County was one of six home League defeats on the trot. Sexton then sent for Gerry Francis, his former captain at Q.P.R. The boat was steadied; City completed a double at Old Trafford, reached the sixth round of the Cup and, a week before they went to The Dell, thrashed Sunderland 6-1 for their biggest win in the top division.

Southampton were fighting for a UEFA Cup place and Coventry had lost only once in 11 games since going out of the Cup. The match was 11 minutes old at the Dell when Steve Hunt crossed and Whitton volleyed City ahead. After a further 11 minutes, Kevin Keegan slid the ball past a hesitant Les Sealey for an equaliser. Despite the blaze of attacking soccer, there were no more goals until 2 minutes before half-time when Hunt created an opening for Hateley. City went in 2-1 up but the Saints were level again a couple of minutes after the break when Keith Cassells glanced a header in from Steve Williams' free-kick. Within 10 minutes, however, City had scored twice to put themselves 4-2 up. Hateley tricked Ivan Golac on the left and put the ball past Ivan Katalinic with a low left-foot shot. Then, Whitton outpaced Chris Nicholl in the heart of the Southampton defence before scoring with an explosive shot from a narrow angle. Straight from the kick-off, Alan Ball ran through and pulled a goal back with a 30-yard shot. On 68 minutes, Cassells made it 4-4 with a delicate chip from the edge of the box. Worse was to come when, 6 minutes from time, Keegan beat City's offside trap to put the Saints ahead for the first time in the match. Although City still had chances, it looked too late. But with the seconds trickling away, Hateley completed his first senior hat-trick by squeezing in an equaliser from an acute angle to bring it to 5-5.

It had been a wonderful match and one that Joe Mercer graciously described as the best he had seen since the 1930s.

Coventry City v. Liverpool

10 December 1983
Highfield Road
Football League Division One
Coventry City 4 Liverpool 0

The improved form at the end of the 1981/82 season did not carry very far into the autumn. Gates dropped, the entertainment was poor and the *Coventry Evening Telegraph* was moved to publish an editorial under the headline 'A Vision blurred,' in which it described Jimmy Hill as 'out of touch with the people who like to watch football'.

It had all been so different. In April 1975, J.H. accepted an invitation to return to Coventry as unpaid managing director. In the club programme, he reminded supporters of a comment he had once made:

> 'You can beat a team, but you can't beat a team and a city.' I said that once when I was manager of Coventry City. We proved it to be true then and I have never stopped believing it since. If I can play a part in restoring the unique atmosphere that existed in this city during those exciting years, then I will know that the decision to accept the board's invitation to join them was the right one... Finally may I say how excited I am to be back at THE football club again, looking towards a bright and exciting future and, with your help and backing, we shall do it again.

Many of us were very stirred by that. Jimmy Hill was a man of conviction, an impressive communicator, a superb salesman. This was a person who had tempted football from its ghetto, opened its eyes to the future, and propelled the game into the consciousness and living rooms of a new, wider generation. He had fought for the rights of his fellow players and galvanised 'a team and a city'. If he rode round the pitch on horseback, we recognised it for what it was but we were also inspired by the sureness and self-belief for which it spoke. The years of austerity had peeled away, both in the city and at the football club. And now the hero was coming home.

Hill became chairman of Coventry City in 1980. On 27 February 1981, the directors of the North American Soccer League approved the relocation of the Detroit Express franchise, in which Coventry had invested, to Washington DC. He said:

> The venture was funded by the coffers of the World Sports Academy [Hill's company], Gary Lemmen, and by an investment of $500,000 from Coventry City Football Club. The Coventry board and I envisaged the advantages of sharing in an enterprise that could give our younger players experience in the USA which would supplement their development and so benefit the club in England. If we could make it work it would close the financial gap between Coventry and its more prosperous First Division rivals.

What went wrong for Hill after his elevation to the chairmanship was not in itself the failure of Washington Diplomats, or the all-seater stadium or the Sky Blue Connexion. It was that supporters could not be persuaded to believe in the integrity of such projects. The pursuit of them seemed increasingly to be at the expense of the team. 'THE football club' was their club, and when Garry Thompson was sold to West Brom it was the last straw. Even the manager questioned the motives.

Dave Sexton.

The club also succeeded in alienating itself from the *Evening Telegraph*, when Hill tried to prevent action pictures being taken from the main stand side. He did not want the tiers of empty seats in the Sky Blue Stand to be visible.

In May 1983, Hill left the board. 'If a chairman is to be held responsible for playing success or failure, or indeed monotonous competence, I am prepared to stand up and be counted,' said Hill. But the board and the public were unhappy. There had also been unease at Hill's involvement in a trip to South Africa the previous summer which had earned him a place on SANROCS's blacklist.

The most poignant thing was that the apostle appeared to have lost touch with his flock. Of course, the agenda – both economically and on account of the undermining effect of hooliganism – was far less straightforward than when J.H. had ridden his horse round the pitch but, sadly, mutual trust evaporated. Nevertheless, misgivings about Jimmy Hill's stewardship will always be balanced by gratitude and respect for his rare qualities as a manager. His achievement had been in so vitally manifesting the vision that he and Derrick Robins set out. He was the beacon in the development of the club from Provincial Rep to West End status.

Hill's successor was Ian Jamieson. He had played ten years at wing half for City in the 1950s and joined the board in 1973. In 1983, he also became chairman of Courtaulds.

From fifth position in February, City collapsed, taking only 3 points from 13 matches. On the Tuesday after the fall of Hill, the Sky Blues – inspired by teenager John Hendrie – won at Stoke. Luton's defeat forty-eight hours later meant that City went into their final game safe from relegation. Sexton was then sacked on the last day of the season. He was replaced by Bobby Gould who had been cutting his teeth in management with Bristol Rovers.

The players were disenchanted by the casting out of Sexton, but for so many of them it was now of little relevance. Many of the contracts which Hill had negotiated were due to expire at the same time. The change in personnel was hardly as great as in 1926, or 2003 for that matter, but the trafficking of players in and out of Highfield Road in the summer of 1983 was certainly exceptional. Mark Hateley went to Portsmouth and within a year signed for Milan for more than five times the £190,000 Coventry received from Pompey. Three years later, he gracelessly wrote himself out of City affections forever:

> It was a good club for a young player to start his career. They didn't care how young you were – if you were good enough, you got your chance. Beyond that, I've nothing good to say about them. They had no ambition. When I saw all the good players leaving, it was obvious that Coventry were a dead-end club. I think they always will be. Getting out was the best thing I did.

Danny Thomas, who had just become the second Coventry player to play for England, was signed by Tottenham for £300,000. Steve Whitton was transferred to West Ham, Paul Dyson to Stoke, and out went Les Sealey, Jim Melrose and Gerry Francis – the five of them for a total of just over £500,000. The biggest sale was Gary Gillespie, who was bought by Liverpool for £325,000.

Of the team that finished the season in May, only 'Harry' Roberts, Peter Hormantschuk and Ian Butterworth ran out at Watford at the end of August. However, Daly, Hendrie, Hunt, Jacobs and Suckling remained on the books and continued to contribute to a varying degree.

The task facing Bobby Gould in his first weeks as a First Division manager was monumental. He needed to go shopping and to go shopping fast. It was a bit like a rush round 'Woolies' on the way to work. His knowledge and nose for players in the lower divisions led him to sign Micky Adams (Gillingham), Dave Bamber (Blackpool), Michael Gynn (Peterborough), Trevor Peake (Lincoln) and, a few months later, a left-back from Wealdstone, Stuart Pearce. Nicky Platnauer and Graham Withey re-joined him from Bristol Rovers. Sam Allardyce (Tampa Bay Rowdies) and a former Yugoslavia goalkeeper, Raddy Avramovic (Inter Montreal), were fished back from across the Atlantic. There were also some who rang a bell: Cardiff's one-time Manchester City winger Dave Bennett, a young Tottenham striker called Terry Gibson and the Manchester United midfielder Ashley Grimes. Nearly £750,000 was spent that summer. Gould had thrown new players into the air like confetti. Would they compliment each other? Roberts, whom Gould appointed as captain, said: 'The bookies reckon we are the biggest relegation certainties of all time. Well, we're going to surprise a lot of people.'

The fact that Gould was able to put the pieces together, and so quickly, was an enormous tribute to his personality and motivational skills. Trouble had been festering backstage. The growing disaffection of players, culminating in frustrating and frustrated contract negotiations, created ill-feeling. Gould arrived in the middle of all this.

Talbot abruptly pulled the plug on their sponsorship. It fell to Gould to provide a sense of leadership at a time of turmoil. As someone with Coventry City in his bones, he was well suited to the task.

A 4-2 win at Luton at the beginning of December put City fifth in the League. Gould had worked miracles so far but the visit of Champions and League leaders Liverpool would surely sort out his unlikely group of travellers. This was the Liverpool of Neal, Hansen and Lawrenson, of Souness, Dalglish and Rush. But after only a minute, Coventry were ahead. Platnauer pounced when Grobbelaar failed to hold Gibson's shot. Nineteen minutes had gone when Bamber, who was

Gordon Milne and Jimmy Hill.

causing the Liverpool defence problems in the air, headed the ball down for Gibson to score a second. Just before half-time, Gibson's bullet of a shot from a half-chance on the edge of the area made it 3. It defied belief; Liverpool had only conceded 9 goals in their first 17 matches. In the second half, despite Liverpool's best efforts, it was the Sky Blues who came closest to scoring with Grobbelaar having to save well from Daly and Gibson. Six minutes from time, City made it 4-0. Gibson chased a clearance, the awkward bounce deceived Phil Neal, and the tiny striker advanced before lobbing Grobbelaar. Gibson's hat-trick was the first against Liverpool for eleven years.

It was one of Coventry City's most outstanding performances. Joe Fagan tipped the Sky Blues as title contenders.

COVENTRY CITY v. NORWICH CITY

12 May 1984
Highfield Road
Football League Division One
Coventry City 2 Norwich City 1

	P	W	D	L	F	A	W	D	L	F	A	GD	P
14 Norwich City	40	9	8	4	34	20	3	6	10	12	26	0	50
15 Ipswich Town	41	10	4	6	32	22	4	4	13	21	34	-3	50
16 Sunderland	41	8	9	4	26	18	4	4	12	14	35	-13	49
17 West Bromwich Albion	40	9	4	7	27	25	4	5	11	18	35	-15	48
18 Birmingham City	41	7	6	7	19	18	5	5	11	20	32	-11	47
19 Coventry City	41	7	5	8	31	32	5	6	10	24	44	-21	47
20 Stoke City	41	10	4	6	26	23	2	7	12	14	40	-23	47
21 Notts County	40	6	6	8	31	36	4	4	12	18	33	-20	40
22 Wolverhampton Wanderers	41	4	8	9	15	28	2	3	15	12	48	-49	29

For Coventry supporters, New Year and the diminishing weeks of winter bring increased anxiety. The bottom of the table becomes cocooned in the mind, a ghetto of veiled threats and hypotheses. An unexpected draw fuels our optimism, the loss of a six-pointer drives us to despair. We stare into the darkness praying that the cuckoo will sing with the spring.

There was no intimation of this as we revelled into 1984. Bobby Gould's hastily assembled troupe had surprised its audience. In December, to the astonishment of the football world, the Sky Blues had thrashed Liverpool. Despite a Christmas defeat at Nottingham Forest, there were draws with Norwich, Manchester United and Everton. Sunderland were first up in the new year. In driving wind and rain, City won 2-1. Not for the first or last time, Sunderland whined – this time about the conditions – but who cared: we were sixth in the League. The manager of Liverpool had tipped us as title contenders. The outlook was rosy.

A home defeat by Watford appeared a mere distraction from the annual fantasy of the FA Cup. Wolves were beaten in a second replay. Maybe this was going to be our year. When City were knocked out at Sheffield Wednesday, it began – as often – to worm its way into the players' confidence. City took only 2 points from 11 matches in the wretched run that followed. The Sky Blues slumped to seventeenth. Wolves, dead but not quite buried at the foot of the table, made their third visit of the season to Highfield Road. In front of a sixth of the number of people who attended the great match in 1967, Mick Ferguson – playing his first game in the First Division for a year – headed the winner.

Almost two years to the day after City and Southampton had shared a ten-goal thriller, the two teams served up ten more goals at the Dell. This time, the thrill was a little less evenly balanced. In the second half, City conceded six goals in the space of 33 minutes. It was a nightmare debut for Lloyd McGrath. The 8-2 defeat was City's heaviest in the League since 1930.

A 5-0 thrashing at Anfield, with Ian Rush scoring four, was an embarrassing reminder of that day in December when everything had looked so different. The sense of foreboding was complete.

Birmingham, Coventry and Stoke were locked on 47 points. At St Andrews, the Blues took on Southampton. Stoke could not have asked for a more sympathetic assignment than Wolves at home.

Bobby Gould and Ian Jamieson.

Norwich opened the scoring against City after 35 minutes with a penalty from John Deehan. We were staring at the abyss. How critical it was for City to immediately claw their way back. The mighty figure of Mick Ferguson was responsible. Ferguson was a throwback to City's goal-happy days in the 1970s, when his career was yet to be punctured by injuries. He was transferred to Everton at the beginning of the 1981/82 season and later joined Birmingham. He was doing little more at St Andrews than drawing his pay cheque when Bobby Gould came with a request to take him on loan. Birmingham were perfectly amenable. Why shouldn't they be? Ferguson was on the shelf, almost forgotten. It didn't even cross their minds that he could play a major part in helping to send them down. It was his equaliser, when City swept towards the Kop end almost from the restart, that turned the game.

However, it was one of the bleakest of half-times. The news from other grounds was not encouraging. If it all stayed the same, you knew that when you returned to the bar or the gents at the end of the match you would be supporting a Second Division club.

The minute hand was about to start its ascent again when City won a corner. All of a sudden, the Sky Blues were ahead. Dave Bennett twisted amd scored.

The depression that had slowly devoured our winter was beginning to lift. We were coming into the straight. However, like a childhood scare on the ghost-train, the biggest fright was yet to come. With only four minutes to go, Robert Rosario had time to admire the gaps in the Coventry defence before planting his header, like Satan filling a Christmas stocking. But Rosario misjudged it. Instead, the ball struck the inside of the post and rebounded into the hands of Perry Suckling who was standing motionless on his line. The minute hand stopped to admire the nonchalance of it all. A few minutes later, the whistle went. The cuckoo was starting to sing.

COVENTRY CITY v. EVERTON

26 May 1985
Highfield Road
Football League Division One
Coventry City 4 Everton 1

	P	W	D	L	F	A	W	D	L	F	A	GD	P
19 Norwich City	42	9	6	6	28	24	4	4	13	18	40	-18	49
20 Coventry City	41	10	3	7	25	21	4	2	15	18	42	-20	47
21 Sunderland	42	7	6	8	20	26	3	4	14	20	36	-22	40
22 Stoke City	42	3	3	15	18	41	0	5	16	6	50	-67	17

We stood in the station bar, talking black-humouredly about all the journeys we would be making to unfamiliar grounds. The floodlights were still blazing behind us, indifferent to the implications they illuminated. City had just drawn 0-0 at Ipswich. With Norwich's unexpected victory at Chelsea, it left the Sky Blues needing to win their last 3 matches to stay up. One of those matches was against Everton, already crowned Champions. It was out of the question. We didn't even consider it.

Steve Ogrizovic and Brian Kilcline were newcomers to the City team that season and Coventry-born John Poynton, resident in Jersey, had succeeded Ian Jamieson as the chairman. The *Coventry Evening Telegraph* paid tribute to Jamieson:

> Most of all, Jamieson's one year reign will be remembered for bringing the club back to the supporters. Gone was the arrogance that distanced it from the people of the city - and in its place all the effort the new management team could muster to seek better relations with the local community.

Poynton enabled Bobby Gould to buy Peter Barnes, Cyrille Regis and David Bowman but a series of poor and porous performances stretched his patience and, after Christmas, Gould was sacked. The new incumbent was Don Mackay, the assistant Gould had recruited in September.

Three days after the Ipswich game, City went to relegated Stoke who had only won 3 and drawn 8 of their 41 fixtures. Stuart Pearce's 66th minute penalty proved enough but it looked all over 6 minutes from time when Stoke were awarded a penalty themselves after Regis was deemed to have fouled Paul Dyson. Ian Painter, another player to represent both clubs, struck his kick powerfully, but the ball caught the underside of the bar and bounced out. On the following Thursday at Highfield Road, a late volley from Brian Kilcline saw off a combative Luton. Everything was set for Sunday morning with all to play for. It was church-going time and so long after the official end of the League season that there were only a few weeks to go to the solstice. Everton were denied the double at Wembley the previous weekend having just won the European Cup-Winners Cup. If they were jaded, it was understandable.

'Groin strains' kept out Andy Gray and Peter Reid who had internationals pending. Others too were imjured but Everton posed a formidable challenge for any team, let alone one in Coventry's position. The Sky Blues got off to the best possible start with a goal after four minutes. Kilcline met Pearce's lofted free-kick with a nod-on to Regis who headed the ball into the corner. With seventeen minutes gone, Terry Gibson's defence-splitting pass was turned on by Regis to Micky Adams who placed a shot past Neville Southall. Despite a goal from Paul Wilkinson just before half-time, City restored their two-goal lead immediately after the interval, Regis tucking in the

Ipswich Town 0 Coventry City 0, 14 May 1985.

rebound from a fierce Gibson shot. Everton were missing Reid's authority in midfield where the wiry Kenny Hibbitt was running the show for City. Twelve minutes from time, the impish Gibson darted onto a long through ball from Pearce and volleyed a fourth, bringing his season's tally to 19.

The unlikely, the incredible, had happened. Stuart Pearce, through the ventriloquism of an autobiography entitled *Psycho,* wrote:

> You could smell the booze on the breath of the Everton players. We were sure they had been out on the Saturday night to celebrate. We were trying our hearts out but if the game had been played a month earlier when they were chasing championship points they would have wiped the floor with us.

Weakened as Everton were, it was a performance of terrific conviction from the Sky Blues. It is strange to recall what a pivotal game it was for Cyrille Regis. Since his much-vaunted transfer from West Bromwich, he had scored only 3 goals in 31 games. 'This has to be one of the most satisfying days of my career. I've had something of a nightmare time here and I was aware that if we had gone down the fans would have blamed me for my lack of goals. And they would have been right,' said Regis. John Poynton enthused: 'These goals from Regis wipe out the transfer fee.'

The season had finished in a straggle like runners in a marathon. Norwich were in a similar position to Coventry in 1969, except for the different ending. While City fans celebrated into the summer afternoon, questions were being asked about the fairness of such important issues being settled fifteen days after the scheduled end to the season.

The loneliest man was Ken Brown, the Norwich City manager. Many at Norwich spent the match biting their nails next to the radio, but Brown decided to take his dog for a walk along the beach.

Coventry City v. Queens Park Rangers

3 May 1986
Highfield Road
Football League Division One
Coventry City 2 Queens Park Rangers 1

	P	W	D	L	F	A	W	D	L	F	A	GD	P
17 Ipswich Town	41	8	5	8	20	24	3	3	14	12	30	-22	41
18 Coventry City	41	5	5	10	29	34	5	5	11	17	36	-24	40
19 Oxford United	40	6	7	6	30	25	3	5	13	28	53	-20	39
20 Leicester City	41	6	8	6	33	35	3	4	14	19	41	-24	39
21 Birmingham City	41	5	2	13	13	24	3	3	15	17	48	-42	29
22 West Bromwich Albion	41	3	8	9	19	33	1	4	16	14	53	-53	24

Oh no, not again. For the third year running, City went into their last match with relegation threatening to grab them by the 'short and curlies'.

After coming from two goals down to beat Southampton at Highfield Road on 22 February, the Sky Blues slumped, and scored only three goals – all from Pickering – in the 10 games leading up to the Q.P.R. one. In 5 of the games they failed to score at all. Events came to a head at Anfield. A 5-0 thrashing was testimony as much to Liverpool brilliance as to Coventry incompetence, but it forced the resignation of Don Mackay. George Curtis and John Sillett were put in temporary charge. Curtis emerged from the boardroom and Sillett from working with aspiring talent at the training ground. Mackay's position had become untenable. However, the appointment of new management, with only 3 games left to play and the team fourth from bottom, came out of desperation more than hope. All 3 of City's remaining fixtures were against teams enjoying good campaigns.

The pre-season, normally a time for keeping fingers crossed over injuries to relaxed and sun-drenched muscles, had focused on a confrontation between Mackay and his skipper, Trevor Peake. Matters came to a head in a row over accommodation at the Crystal Palace Sports Centre. Peake was sent home, and relinquished the captaincy.

Stuart Pearce and Ian Butterworth had joined Nottingham Forest but two more pieces of the Cup-winning jigsaw – Brian Borrows and Greg Downs – fell into place. Downs had discovered about relegation when City's extraordinary escape sent Norwich down the year before. Wayne Turner, a midfielder signed from Luton, took over the captaincy.

City struggled from the start, particularly at home. The Southampton win in February was the first at Highfield Road since 6 October, although there were four away victories during this time. Despite the seating being stripped out of the Kop End, attendances dropped and the crowd for the Watford game, 7,478, remains the lowest for a top division match at Highfield Road.

With leaves falling on the rails, City began to put together a little run but Advent brought a series of terrible results, and, by the turn of the year, Brian Kilcline had been installed as captain. John Reason, Derrick Richardson and Ted Stocker joined the board.

The club accepted a £650,000 bid from Manchester United for Terry Gibson. Gibson's alertness and lust for goal had been priceless in his two-and-a-half seasons at Coventry, his record of 51 goals in 111 appearances remarkable under the circumstances. In October and November, he scored in 7 consecutive games. Regis, despite scoring five goals in one League Cup match against Chester,

Trevor Peake.   George Curtis and John Sillett.

managed only the same number in the League all season. Gibson was replaced by Alan Brazil who came in part-exchange. The balance of the cash also bought Nick Pickering and Jim McInally. McInally is still remembered for the magnificent own goal he scored at Highbury when he headed a cross from Graham Rix into his own net.

An instant exit from the FA Cup did not in itself precipitate the collapse in League form, but by Easter Monday a home defeat by Ipswich confirmed another fidgety finish. A few days after the Ipswich game, City sacked their first team coach, Frank Upton.

Coventry supporters may have felt like battle-hardened soldiers, enjoying a last drag before adjusting their helmets, but the moment of truth had not got any easier. After their guardians took control, City beat Luton at Highfield Road and lost at West Ham. On the last day, four teams were vying to join Birmingham and West Brom in descent.

The Sky Blues went a goal down after 28 minutes, John Byrne's shot taking a deflection off Peake. Ten minutes later, up stepped Kilcline to blast a free-kick in the powerful and unerring manner that was his trademark and City were level. The referee was warming his whistle for half-time. Before it could reach Mr Wilson's lips, Dave Bennett tricked his way through the visitors' defence and put City ahead.

Q.P.R. threatened to score for much of the second half and even hit the crossbar. However, City gradually eased their supporters out of their cold sweat and away from the firing-line. Leicester had also won but Ipswich's defeat at Hillsborough meant that beaten Oxford needed to win their last game to stay up. Forty-eight hours later, Oxford put three past Arsenal at the Manor and Ipswich dropped through the floor.

Would City appoint Curtis and Sillett on a permanent basis?

Sheffield Wednesday v. Coventry City

25 October 1986
Hillsborough
Football League Division One
Sheffield Wednesday 2 Coventry City 2

Someone who scores once, and only once, during a career of well over 700 senior games is almost certain to be a goalkeeper. Goalkeepers are as likely to score as cricketers to be dismissed for Hit the Ball Twice or Handled the Ball – Len Hutton was given out in a Test match for Obstructing the Field. When it happens, it is either from a flukeish punt or in a kitchen-sink role when everything needs to be thrown at the opposition. Jimmy Glass famously saved Carlisle from dropping out of the League when he manifested himself like a phantom in the Plymouth penalty-area. In January 1984, the Watford 'keeper Steve Sherwood scored against the Sky Blues, his kick taking Raddy Avramovic by surprise in the high wind.

Nowadays, expediency pushes the techniques of sport to the limit. Rugby players pick each other up in the line-out in order to catch a high throw-in, cricketers routinely go into a slide to field the ball. But the idea of a goalkeeper honing his scoring skills stretches credulity. Is there no stone unturned? In the week before the Hillsborough match, discussion at the Ryton training ground turned to the problems caused by the autumn winds. Jake Findlay, Coventry's reserve 'keeper, spoke admiringly to Steve Ogrizovic of Sheffield Wednesday's Martin Hodge. He observed that Hodge had an occasional tendency to stand well off his line which could make him vulnerable in windy conditions. After training, Findlay persuaded Ogrizovic to go back out. Oggy punted balls from one goal to the other with Findlay taking up a variety of positions close to the opposite 18-yard line.

Hillsborough lies in a valley and on the day of the game the wind was sweeping down from the Wadsley side of it. It was also raining 'cats and dogs'. Oggy was 6 to 8 yards off his line as he stood clasping the ball at the Leppings Lane end. He knew the pitch to be 115 yards long and could assess the strength of the wind at that moment from the angle of the rain under the floodlight in the left-hand corner. Hodge was well off his goal-line. Oggy aimed a huge kick. The ball pitched in front of Hodge and took off over his head, brushing the inside of the left upright. It trickled unassumingly across the line and into the opposite corner of the goal. For a moment there was an eerie silence – 'Was it? Wasn't it?' – then the realisation. Poor Hodge stood with his head bowed. From then on, City fans in the cages at the Leppings Lane end shouted 'Shoot, Shoot!' every time Oggy had the ball.

It was a goal that outlived the significance of the match. Cyrille Regis had scored in the first half for City; Lee Chapman netted twice for Wednesday. The Sky Blues were sixth in the table.

This was the start of an *annus mirabilis* for Ogrizovic. It was fitting that the likes of Diego Maradona and Michel Platini should have the opportunity to play against Oggy when he was selected for the Football League against The Rest of the World at Wembley the following August. Oggy's modesty led him to deny that his goal had involved anything other than chance. His skill, sportsmanship, loyalty and professionalism place him among the very finest players ever to have represented the club. His record of 601 first-team appearances, 246 of them consecutive, is unlikely to be surpassed.

Let us honour this devoted custodian of Coventry. Christopher Robin went down with Alice but shouldn't Oggy be invited to the Palace?

Steve Ogrizovic.

SHEFFIELD WEDNESDAY v. COVENTRY CITY

14 March 1987
Hillsborough
FA Cup Sixth Round
Sheffield Wednesday 1 Coventry City 3

It all began on 30 August 1986. At Folkestone's Cheriton Road, Essex went in to bat against Kent. 'A masterly innings by Gooch, with fine support from Fletcher, kept Essex going against the spin of Underwood', wrote *Wisden*. Just down the road at the Crabble Ground in Dover, where – almost to the day in 1935 – W.H. Ashdown smote an unbeaten 282 on the opening day of Kent's match with Derbyshire, Dover Athletic were playing out a goalless draw against Tunbridge Wells. It was the preliminary round of the Football Association Challenge Cup. The attendance, the fifth highest in 131 preliminary round matches, was 308; Coventry Sporting's official crowd for the visit of Racing Club Warwick was 32, the second lowest.

Dover Athletic scored 3 more goals in the Cup that season than the eventual winners. It was the centenary year of the original Tunbridge Wells club, whose percentage of wins per games played has only recently been surpassed by King's Lynn as the highest in all-time FA Cup results.

Top scorers that day were Metropolitan Police who chalked up an 8-1 win at Chesham United. The most bizarre episode of the round occurred later at Ringmer where the referee called off a replay in extra time due to bad light when Arundel were leading 3-0. Arndel repeated the score when the match was played again, but in just 90 minutes.

Over 160 of the 504 FA Cup entrants had already been eliminated by the time Essex won the County Championship on 16 September. Caernarfon Town had won the first of 6 ties. Only one other team would win as many.

On 10 January 1987, the First and Second Division clubs entered the fray. At Highfield Road, Coventry City entertained Bolton Wanderers. Bolton – Cup winners as recently as 1958 – would find themselves in the Fourth Division in a few months time, with Wolves, another fallen giant, among their opponents.

Another dour season had been in prospect when the Sky Blues ran out at Upton Park for their opening fixture. We had heard of David Phillips, a Wales international midfielder signed from Manchester City, but where were the goals going to come from? Supporters' only recollection of Scunthorpe striker Keith Houchen was his winning penalty in a Cup-tie for York City against Arsenal. Ian Painter from Stoke was to be as tainted by fitness problems as the outgoing Alan Brazil. However, George Curtis and John Sillett, now confirmed in their managerial roles, were to make two major tactical adjustments. The under-scoring Cyrille Regis persuaded them to release him from the target-man role in order to make more use of his ball control, acceleration and ability to hold up the ball. It became their most important managerial decision. The dribbling and shooting skills of Dave Bennett were then maximised by playing him alongside Regis in a 4-4-2 formation.

In October, Dean Emerson – a tigerish and talented midfielder – was signed from Rotherham, having made a big impression against City in the League Cup. Few Coventry players down the years have so quickly asserted themselves in the stitching of the team.

The attractiveness and finesse of City's football found its maturity at Highfield Road at Christmas. In a match that easily emulated any puff of panatellas, the Sky Blues twice came from behind to beat Tottenham. Regis made it 4-3 with City's last kick of the match. The spirit and excitement were a portent of the extraordinary weeks to come.

Cyrille Regis,
Coventry City
and England.

Supporters had only just begun to trust that something rather special was developing. There were still only 12,044 at Highfield Road for the Bolton game. Bolton's manager, Phil Neal, had dropped himself. Greg Downs, from 25 yards out, opened the scoring from Brian Borrows' free-kick. Further goals from Regis and Bennett gave the Sky Blues a 3-0 victory.

Being drawn at Manchester United in the fourth round would certainly have guaranteed the excitement of the bank manager, but many people also felt that a good result was within City's reach. United had already lost 4 League games at Old Trafford. Alex Ferguson was the new manager, Gordon Strachan and Terry Gibson two of his team. George Curtis returned with his players from a week in Spain and blithely announced to the cameras: 'Our name is on the Cup.' It was Keith Houchen who gave credence to his words. Houchen was only playing because of injury to Bennett, but 20 minutes into the match, with the ball bobbing as if on a ping-pong table, he stabbed home the only goal of the match from a yard out.

This time, the draw was a little kinder with an away tie at Second Division Stoke City. Twelve First Division clubs had already fallen and the draw guaranteed that another three would not finish. It was hardly a case of Foinavon in the Grand National, but the realisation was growing that this closely-knit Coventry side were a good bet for the Cup.

Memories of City's desperate win at the Victoria Ground two years before were still fresh in the mind. On a previous occasion, the shouts of someone accidentally locked in the gents had gone unheard until the end of the game. Maybe he was still on the throne when they came to demolish the ground.

Stoke had crashed 4-1 at The Hawthorns a week before, ending a 14-match unbeaten run that included a 7-2 victory against Leeds. City were without the suspended Emerson for the first time but won with a 72nd-minute goal from Michael Gynn. Gynn, dipping and scudding with nervous energy and with something of the Chaplin in his face, was improvising to increasing effect and proving himself worthy of more than his usual walk-on role. The unmarked Phillips could not properly control Nick Pickering's cross but Gynn was there to put it away.

A Lloyd McGrath goal gave City an inspiring victory in atrocious conditions at home to Sheffield Wednesday a week before the two teams met in the Sixth Round. But victory came at a cost. The injury sustained by Emerson as a result of a bad tackle by Megson was to keep him out until the end of October. At least City could recall Bennett.

There had been 4,000 City fans at Old Trafford, 8,000 at Stoke; 15,000 would take over the Leppings Lane end at Hillsborough. The euphoria of the Cup run was sweeping the city.

The most recent of Coventry's four previous quarter-final appearances had been in 1982 when Regis scored a superb goal for West Brom. City's only win in 3 FA Cup-ties at Hillsborough had been in 1911. The Owls were unbeaten at home in the FA Cup for fourteen years.

There are abiding memories of Cyrille Regis at Hillsborough, casting a crossfield ball like a yo-yo or feeding his team with that obstinate skill and determination, but especially of his goal. We had the perfect view of it looking down from the Leppings Lane End. Bennett unleashed him and Regis drew our eyes, the perfect vision of a centre forward bearing down on the far goal with the field his own. Hodge advanced and the goal magnified with Cyrille's deadly finish.

A Sheffield Wednesday equaliser finally arrived in the 67th minute when Gary Megson forced his way through to score. For a time, Wednesday were on top.

With twelve minutes to go, City were about to make a substitution, pulling off Houchen and pushing Bennett up front. Aside from his goal at Old Trafford, Houchen had scored only once since establishing a place in the team after Christmas. In the very next attack, however, he made himself irreplaceable when he scored with a deflected left-foot shot from just inside the area. It was the greatest substitution that never was. Five minutes later, Houchen scored again. A headed clearance caught him right in the face, bringing tears to his eyes as he struck the ball sweetly into the far corner from almost the same position as his first goal.

Houchen was not the only one in tears. 'I could see men crying, I could actually see them crying,' he said. The hero had dropped to his knees, fists clenched, in front of grown men for whom it was all too much.

Right: 'Greggie, Greggie, Greggie Downs, got no hair, we don't care'.

Below: Cyrille Regis scores City's opening goal.

COVENTRY CITY v. LEEDS UNITED

12 April 1987
Hillsborough
FA Cup Semi-Final
Coventry City 3 Leeds United 2

The pilgrimage swept northwards in the Sunday morning sun. Cars crammed the M1 with a sea of scarves swirling from every window to match the brightness of the sky.

At the Sheffield exit, we ground to a halt. Passengers, full of tea no doubt, leapt from their coaches. We were relieved that the 12.15 p.m. kick-off had been put back a quarter-of-an-hour. What a tragedy such a decision would not be taken two years later.

This was the draw we had prayed for as we huddled round our radios. We had certainly earned it, on the road at Old Trafford and Stoke, and already at Hillsborough in the quarter-finals. Watford were Tottenham's opponents in the other semi-final. Spurs crushed them 4-1 but they went on to finish ninth in the League. Leeds were Second Division, with half an eye on what was to be an unsuccessful play-off.

Leeds looked anything but Second Division in the opening 15 minutes as the Sky Blues were gripped by stage fright. It was Steve Ogrizovic, playing the game of his life, who kept Coventry in the match. How Watford could have wished for him the previous day at Villa Park when their stand-in 'keeper Gary Plumley – son of the former Coventry secretary – was deemed to have cost his club dearly.

It had been little surprise that Leeds, who were dictating the early pace, took the lead after 14 minutes. David Rennie, later to play for Coventry, headed in a corner from Micky Adams, whom Leeds had bought from City at the beginning of the year.

Oggy, who had beaten out a close-range header in the second minute, made a superb point-blank save minutes after Leeds scored. Gradually, the Sky Blues steadied themselves. Regis, who had twice been a loser at the semi-final stage, made three glaring misses in a nine-minute spell. Was the memory of his failure to cut out Rennie's header playing on his mind?

In the dressing room at half-time, Lloyd McGrath, for whom the expression 'quietly spoken' could have been coined, burst into a rendition of 'Here we go'. Soon he was joined by all his team-mates. The City players emerged with their confidence reborn.

It was the introduction of Gynn 15 minutes into the second half in place of the injured Pickering that saw the game begin to turn. Minutes later, the Leeds defender Ormsby attempted to allow the ball to run over the line for a goalkick, only to be left stranded by Bennett's determined challenge. Chasing a seemingly lost cause, Bennett crossed and Gynn finished it off. There were 27,000 City fans who hit the roof.

Nine minutes later, there was another eruption as Houchen, the match-winner at Old Trafford and scorer of two goals in the quarter-final, put City in front. Gynn's run created panic in the Leeds defence; Houchen coolly collected the ball and rounded his old Orient teammate Mervyn Day before finding the net with a low left foot shot. The hero was buried by his teammates, who echoed the roar of the gigantic bank of sky blue in front of them, shouting: 'Roy, Roy.' It was Melchester Rovers and this was the front page.

We were nearly there. But the game took another unexpected turn 7 minutes from time when Downs and Gynn failed to stop the tireless Andy Ritchie from putting in a great right-wing cross. Substitute Keith Edwards headed home from close range with his first touch of the ball. 'A

Hillsborough, 1989.

match that was always memorable has now become wonderful,' enthused Martin Tyler from the commentary box. Roger Milford blew for full-time. One or two Leeds players, with the excitement of the equaliser, had forgotten that there would be extra time. How galling that must have been. Coventry too had been so close but so far. This was no longer from the pages of a comic. It was to be the most crucial peptalk of John Sillett's life.

Ten minutes into extra time and it was 3-2, 3-2 to City. Adams fouled Bennett and Gynn's free-kick was headed into the crowded goalmouth by Regis. The lurking Houchen's left-foot shot was blocked but Bennett pounced on the ball to score. It proved to be the winner and it was appropriate that it should be scored by Dave Bennett. He had taken the laces out of Adams' boots that afternoon, and made the first goal and so nearly several others.

There could have been another twist as extra time ebbed away. Ogrizovic, arms outstretched in front of him, dived full-length at the feet of Edwards. Just as Oggy had kept City alive in the early minutes, it was this absurdly brave save that ensured that Coventry City would be playing at Wembley. Gordon Banks was effusive in his praise of Ogrizovic: 'On this season's form he is the best keeper in the country... he has taken on a coating of extra-special skill and brilliance that separates the great goalkeepers from the good ones.'

It had been a semi-final of rare quality, of fluctuation and skilfulness, of high resolve but sportsmanship. Coventry City had booked their place in the wider public consciousness.

The sun and warmth suggested summer. It had been a joyous occasion, beautifully organised and policed. How incomprehensible that the semi-final at Hillsborough two years later could result in such horror. On this occasion, as the fans collapsed into their coaches, it was with mere exhaustion. The *Coventry Evening Telegraph* wrote:

> The city feels young again today. It has a skip in its step, a smile on its face and a tear in its eye. It has dreamed the impossible dream and woken up to find it reality. Coventry City at Wembley... the boyhood ambition of so many fans long ago and now realised in their dotage. Nobody was talking about anything else today. And how marvellous that is for the city. Not since the sixties has a Midland team got to the Cup Final. The prosperous place it was then is very much different now for Coventry as for the rest of the region. The Sky Blues' lusty victory on a glorious spring day in Yorkshire will give people something to cheer and be proud of. Yet the city is just starting to believe in itself again and soccer success can symbolise it. The people's game has the power to do that as anyone who's been in the factory on the Monday after a big result will testify. George Curtis, John Sillett and their players have lifted the city's morale sky-high. What was possible for them against all the odds is possible now for us all.

Coventry City v. Charlton Athletic

13 May 1987
Highfield Road
FA Youth Cup Final Second Leg
Coventry City 1 Charlton Athletic 0

Gary Marshall did not go on to make even a ripple in the professional game. However, on the Wednesday before Wembley it was his perfect cross, headed in by Steve Livingstone in the 113th minute, that set Coventry on the way to completing the first half of the FA Youth Cup and FA Cup double. Arsenal in 1971 and Everton in 1984 remain the only other clubs to achieve this.

The triumph of the Youth Team, coached by Mick Coop, came at the end of a mammoth run of 13 games, 7 more than their seniors. Having drawn the first leg 1-1 at Selhurst Park with a goal from Craig Middleton (his twin brother Lee was also in the team), the Sky Blues took the trophy in front of a 12,142 crowd at Highfield Road. City, exempted until the second round, had beaten West Bromwich and Southampton in replays, Oldham in a second replay, Watford, and then Manchester City in a replay after their two-legged semi-final had ended level on aggregate. The gangly, ginger-haired Livingstone finished as top scorer with six goals.

The first FA Youth Cup Final was in 1953. Manchester United, including Colman, Edwards, Pegg and Whelan – all so soon to be mourned – beat Wolverhampton Wanderers 9-3 (7-1 and 2-2) on aggregate; they went on to win the first five finals. Ninety-three clubs entered the first competition and were grouped together in convenient geographical areas. In an early game, Manchester United put twenty-three goals past Nantwich, whose goalkeeper they still considered good enough to sign up after the game. Huntley and Palmer's of Reading reached the semi-finals. Coventry City first entered in 1955/56 and reached the third round before losing at mighty Wolves.

Matt Busby grasped the importance of making youth a priority. Young footballers, who had gazed out middle-aged from generations of team groups, suddenly took on a v-necked and virile appearance.

Jimmy Hill was one of many to follow Busby's example by extending his club's scouting network. In 1965, two Cambridge schoolboys were among the intake of new City apprentices. One of them was Willie Carr.

In the late 1960s, when diet and fitness were yet to catch up with the pace and stamina demanded by the modern game, many players were nearing the end of their careers even before they turned thirty. Outstanding youngsters such as Carr, with the school leaving age still at fifteen, were often beginning to establish regular first-team places by the time they were eighteen. First-team squads were smaller and clubs were relying increasingly on the production line of a youth scheme.

Coventry made their first appearance in the FA Youth Cup Final in 1968. Carr was absent from both games on first-team duty but City beat Burnley 2-1 in the first leg at Highfield Road. Burnley, who were producing a more consistent stream of outstanding young talent than any other club in the country, took the trophy 3-2 on aggregate. Jeff Blockley, Graham Paddon and Trevor Gould were the other members of the City team to make significant careers in the game. The other Cambridge schoolboy, Don Peachey, went to Australia.

Under Bob Dennison as chief scout, City developed a wider and keener scouting network than ever before. It does not necessarily follow though that outstanding youngsters make a successful team. Gordon Strachan pointed out that it can be a disadvantage to have too many at one time: young players need room to breathe.

FA Youth Cup Squad, 1970. From left to right, back row: Jack Leavers (coaching assistant), Alan Dugdale, Neil Merrick, Bob Stockley, David Icke, Jim Holmes, Joe Fillipi, Noel Finglas, Tommy Howard, Ron Farmer (coach). Front row: Ivan Crossley, Les Cartwright, Alan Green, Colin Randell, Dennis Mortimer (captain), Mick McGuire, Trevor Smith, Bob Parker, Johnny Stevenson.

However, the 1970 team – under the tutelage of Ronnie Farmer – was one of the best Under-18s club sides ever seen in this country. Having won both legs of their semi-final against Manchester United, the Sky Blues lost to Tottenham in a second replay after the two-legged final finished level. Graeme Souness – who was sent off in the third game for trying to kick Mortimer, Ray Clarke – later to be Coventry's European scout, and Steve Perryman were members of the Spurs side.

One of the rising stars was Bobby Parker. Favourable comparisons were already being drawn with Bobby Moore but Parker never compensated for a certain slowness and one-footedness as adequately as the great man. Jimmy Holmes, Dennis Mortimer, Alan Dugdale, Les Cartwright, Alan Green and Mick McGuire were also all destined to make their mark in the First Division. David Icke, Johnny Stevenson and Colin Randell made it to the bench, even if not the pitch, during City's only European adventure. Randell went on to make 437 League appearances in the lower divisions. Icke kept goal in 37 of Hereford United's inaugural League games. Such is the poignancy of unfulfilled dreams that right-back Ivan Crossley, who as a member of the 1968 team had been rated the club's outstanding prospect, was the only one besides Stevenson and Trevor Smith never to graduate to League football.

By the late 1980s, rules governing the signing of schoolboys had become much stricter. No longer could a club risk a fistful of greenbacks to secure a parental commitment as in the bad old days. Scouting and providing for youngsters had become a major expense, making bargain-hunting in the lower divisions – so successful for City under Bobby Gould – a more profitable approach. It is only now, with the coming of Academy schemes, that things have come full circle.

City reached the Youth Cup Final again in 1999 and 2000, losing on aggregate 9-0 to a magnificent West Ham team and 5-1 to Arsenal.

Of the 1987 side, only Tony Dobson, who made 54 League appearances for City, and Steve Livingstone, whose four-goal salvo against Sunderland put City into the League Cup semi-final in 1990, were to make any considerable contribution to City's first team.

It was appropriate that the youngsters should join the open-top bus tour of the city on the day after their seniors had completed the double at Wembley. At the reception at the Civic Centre, some of them – Gary Marshall included perhaps – were popping champagne corks as if at a grand prix.

COVENTRY CITY v. TOTTENHAM HOTSPUR

16 May 1987
Wembley Stadium
FA Cup Final
Coventry City 3 Tottenham Hotspur 2

The restored bells of the bombed cathedral rang out for the first time in a hundred years. At the end of morning service in the new cathedral, the congregation applauded and cheered as choirboys donned sky blue scarves over their surplices and sang out in exultation. Later in the day, nearly a quarter-of-a-million people – most of the population of Coventry – crowded into the Sunday drizzle to rejoice.

The luxury hotel overlooking Pool Meadow had been offering a special deal for people wanting to avoid the Cup Final. Not surprisingly, there were no takers. For this was more than just a football match, a great one at that. It was more than romance over the triumph of the underdog, more even than civic pride at the greatest day in the local football club's history.

This was about a spirit of community in an age of less and less certainty. For a moment, football transcended its many problems, problems overseen at the time by a government intent on holding the game to account for the wider social evils that bedevilled it.

It was a human allegory, the story of years of getting by and hanging on, of everything then coming together in a marriage of circumstances, personalities and talents – in one extraordinary achievement.

It was the story of Keith Houchen launching himself across the turf to score one of the most spectacular goals ever seen at Wembley Stadium. What a goal that would have been, you thought, pinching yourself to realise that it was not a dream after all. It was in that moment, as Houchen's head made contact to level the scores at 2-2, that the sea of Sky Blues supporters behind the goal – and probably the Tottenham contingent too – realised whose spirit was going to prevail that afternoon.

George Curtis and John Sillett, jigging and galumphing together with the trophy, personified the balance of contrasts and coincidences so vital to success. From the moment of the fourth-round win at Old Trafford and being drawn at Stoke, from having the 'Our name's on the Cup' feeling for the first time, they diligently and enthusiastically kept their team bubbling. More than anything, they fostered an unquenchable spirit as the team relaxed and prepared for each hurdle at the same Dorset hotel, a few miles from Sillett's birthplace in the village of Nomansland. It was a triumph for 'Schnoz', who had returned to the club he had once played for and from which more recently he had been sacked as a coach.

That elusive chemistry of character and ability had been taking shape over many months. Sillett ensured that the preparations for the final were perfect. Realising how few of his players had played at Wembley, he got the permission of the groundsman to train there. Stillett said:

> The ground staff even provided piped crowd noises to give us a sense of the atmosphere. The visit was to protect the players so none of them would be surprised on the day. I think that played a very important part in our winning... We had a superstition that if we saw a bride on the day of the match we would never lose. We were staying in Marlow, and there was a church on the opposite side of the Thames. So on the morning of the match I organised a boat to bring a bride across the river, and she met all the players.

Above left: Dave Bennett equalises – 1-1.

Above right: David Phillips and Michael Gynn.

Right: FA Cup Winners, 1987.

One of the newcomers to Wembley was a brave Brummie boy, Lloyd McGrath, who was to be Man of the Match. The injury-prone McGrath had broken his legs twice over. He never promised much of a pass as he shuffled around the City midfield, but on this day he played the game of his life, tailor-made for man-marking the best passer of them all, Glenn Hoddle.

However, this was not a victory for brutishness over artistry. The Brazil players, watching the match prior to playing England the following Wednesday, were amazed that a player of Dave Bennett's insistent and incisive skill was not in the England team.

Bennett and Regis formed a triangle with Houchen. Coventry hardly broke the bank or the back page when they signed Houchen from Scunthorpe but he possessed the necessary control to create the space for Bennett and Regis.

Cyrille Regis, that athlete of aristocratic touch, bursting with acceleration over the first few yards, of deftness but supreme power, was at the centre of the afternoon. He had grown up in the area and once been turned down as a porter by the hotel next to the stadium. That gravity of balance, that ability to strew opponents like a scythe, had taken early shape in a park just across the hill.

The supporters gave the players a colourful send-off at Highfield Road at their last League game, but injury struck down Brian Borrows. 'Bugsy', maybe a yard too slow for international football, was as accomplished a right-back as any in the British game. Nobody more richly deserved an appearance at Wembley, but he limped off with a knee injury in the second half against Southampton. Thankfully, there was a ready-made replacement in David Phillips, an excellent crosser of the ball, who could fall back from midfield allowing Michael Gynn to come in.

Greg Downs ran on to the field against Southampton, replete with toupee, to the customary chant of 'Greggie, Greggie, Greggie Downs, got no hair, we don't care.' Downs had fought hard to live down the sobriquet he acquired as 'Dodgy' after his transfer from Norwich. Two minutes into the Cup Final though, Chris Waddle beat him inside out to cross for Clive Allen to open the scoring.

Seven minutes later, Downs redeemed himself. His chip into the box was flicked on by Houchen. Bennett pounced in front of Ray Clemence before turning to finish from close range with a hard left-foot shot.

With tentativeness dispelled and half-time in sight, City then fell behind for a second time. Oggy, whose wife had given birth on the Thursday morning, could be forgiven as Hoddle's searching free-kick appeared to cannon off Brian Kilcline's right foot before bouncing into the empty net. The goal was credited to Gary Mabbutt.

We were facing a mountain. At half-time, we stared across the wastes of North London from the balcony of the stadium feeling empty – very empty. We were naive to think that this was really going to be our day, that Coventry City would win the FA Cup... weren't we?

How could we have had such little faith. Just after the hour came that defining moment. Oggy's huge kick was headed on by Regis to Houchen, who instantly controlled the ball and dispatched it to Bennett on the right wing. Bennett cut the cross back for Houchen who had turned and run through. Nicky Pickering, who was standing behind, his Geordie lilt infused with urgency, shouted: 'Dive Houchy, dive.' And dive Houchy did. Even for a stadium that had witnessed an Olympic Games and a World Cup, it was one of the truly great sights. If we did not believe then that the Cup could be ours, we did as the whistle went for the end of normal time. Tottenham's players sank to the ground, Coventry's remained standing. Tottenham were finished.

Graham Rodger replaced the injured Kilcline just before the end of normal time. In the first half of extra time, it was Rodger's pass that led to City's winner. The ball was taken up by the ceaselessly energetic McGrath, whose dipping cross took a deflection off Gary Mabbutt high over Ray Clemence and into the net. Tommy Hutchison, in 1981, remains the only other player to score for both sides in the Cup Final. Gynn and Bennett could have added further to the score but it was enough. Coventry had won the Cup.

This was the 'friendly final', played in a spirit of sportsmanship and refereed with discretion and good humour by Neil Midgley. One moment epitomised it all. The ever-timely Trevor Peake gave Clive Allen a ride on his back as the two of them went for a loose ball. Midgley pulled up the Spurs man for an infringement with Allen airborne on Peake's shoulders. There were grins all round.

In the excitement of City's winner, the club chairman, John Poynton, admitted to a faux pas as he brought the Duchess of Kent to her feet. It was to his and everyone's disappointment that the rightful ban on English clubs in Europe, as a result of the Heysel Stadium tragedy, denied 'Coventry, a club whose supporters are among the best behaved in the League', as one national newspaper leader commented, 'its chance of European glory'.

It had been an exhausting adventure. We felt drained as we came away from the ground, as we had after the semi-final. We needed time to draw breath, time to believe that it really had been Brian Kilcline holding the Cup.

Coventry won valiantly with a performance of fitness, skill and above all, indomitable spirit. John Sillett was an exceptional motivator who sent his players out feeling like giants and who fostered a rare friendship and camaraderie between his players. The *Coventry Evening Telegraph* commented:

Above: Keith Houchen equalises – 2-2.

Coventry, 17 May, 1987.

Brian Kilcline lifts the Cup.

It would be difficult to overestimate the effect of this football match on the spirits of our city... Its footballers have now given proof to those workers whose skills were written off that seemingly impossible dreams are attainable. There is fresh hope in the air today.

The Coventry players enjoyed the night, but paid for it the next day. The club hired an open-top bus for a victory parade round the city. 'We spent six hours on the bus which had no toilet,' said Sillett. 'That was tough after a night of celebration.'

On 16 January 2002, the club brought together the whole Cup-winning team again for the first time since 1987. The jazz-loving Michael Gynn, now a postman, was lost beneath Killer's dreadlocks. Killer now renovates houses in Holmfirth, the home of Nora Batty. There was PC Greg Downs, Steve Sedgley, big Cyrille, without the chest but as godlike as ever – a treasure trove of grateful memories. And you could still sense that team spirit. How we could have done with some of it that night. City had been drawn at home to Spurs in the third round and duly lost 2-0 to a vastly superior side. We had come full circle.

Goal times: Allen (Tottenham) 1 min 51 seconds, Bennett (Coventry) 8 mins 38 seconds, Mabbutt (Tottenham) 40 mins 10 seconds, Houchen (Coventry) 62 mins 42 seconds, Mabbutt o.g. (Coventry) 96 mins 46 seconds.

READING v. COVENTRY CITY

2 March 1988
Elm Park
Simod Cup Semi-Final
Reading 1 Coventry City 1

Eleven weeks after the Cup Final, tens of thousands of Coventry supporters returned to Wembley to watch the Sky Blues contest the Charity Shield with League Champions Everton. The first FA Charity Shield match was played in 1908. Among the beneficiaries of the 1912 game were families of the victims of the Titanic disaster. The event became an informal curtain-raiser to the new season. In 1974, it moved to Wembley where, aside from raising greater sums for charity, it became a portent for the hyperbole of the months ahead. In the Borough of Brent, chanting fans and replica shirts in August seemed as incongruous as cricket at Christmas.

In 1987, the first day of August was particularly hot and sunny. The 88,000 crowd saw Everton win with a goal from Wayne Clarke. Brian Borrows gained some consolation for missing the Cup Final by coming on as a second half substitute for Michael Gynn. Cyrille Regis missed the match through injury, which opened the door for the club's record £780,000 signing, David Speedie.

John Sillett was now manager in his own right as George Curtis had moved up to become managing director. Sillett went out to spend the stocking-full of notes the FA Cup had provided and Speedie's unveiling was a media event. 'For too long this club has shopped at Woolworth's, from now on we'll be shopping at Harrods,' was Sillett's brassy comment. Speedie had scored 3 goals in 22 league appearances for Chelsea the previous season and never as many as his partner, Kerry Dixon. Keith Houchen had scored 2 goals in 20 league appearances for Coventry and Sillett was determined to replace him, despite his 5 goals in the FA Cup. Speedie was a 'name'. Whether his talent was sufficient to compensate for his cussedness remained to be seen and whether it was sensible to break up the triangle in which Houchen was the apex for the success of Regis and Bennett was questionable.

City's first match of the season was against, of all sides, Tottenham Hotspur. Speedie immediately endeared himself with a terrific goal in the 2-1 victory. A poor autumn, with an 11-match run without a win, saw City plummet to seventeenth in the table at the turn of the year. The Sky Blues surrendered the FA Cup in the fourth round at Highfield Road when they could have played all day without getting the ball past Tony Coton in the Watford goal. League Cup defeat came against Luton in a game played at Leicester due to Luton's ban on away fans. City went from 3 October to 13 February without a League win at home, and it was only the unbeaten away run from then till the end of the season that enabled the Sky Blues to finish as high as tenth. Dave Bennett and Lloyd McGrath both sustained broken legs but Brian Borrows and Dean Emerson were restored to full fitness. Young David Smith was beginning to make an impact on the left wing and Steve Sedgley was now established in midfield. Speedie scored only 6 League goals.

In 1985, partly as a consequence of the ban on English clubs in Europe, the FA introduced the Full Members' Cup for First and Second Division clubs. Some clubs shunned it but it was bestowed – to use cricketing parlance – with first-class status. Simod, a sportswear company, became its sponsors in 1987 before the computer company Zenith Data Systems took over in 1992.

There was a joke about the Simod Cup to the effect that the difference between the competition and the ears of *Star Trek*'s Mr Spock was that Spock's ears had a point to them. It is a joke that amplifies the frustration about a season in which the Simod Cup had become City's only aspiration

From left to right:
Nicky Pickering,
Steve Sedgley,
Keith Houchen,
Dave Bennett,
Cyrille Regis,
David Phillips.

and possible compensation. Having beaten Wimbledon and Ipswich at home, the Sky Blues were now one step away from another trip to Wembley. Reading and Elm Park symbolised a world Coventry City had long since left behind. On this drenched evening the last balloons from the previous May were finally burst.

There was a farcical start to proceedings. The City players were on the pitch ready for the eight o'clock kick-off, only to be ushered off for a fifteen-minute wait to allow all of the 15,348 fans to get into the ground. Meanwhile, the Reading team had been informed of the police request and remained in their dressing room. When the two sides finally emerged, it seemed that some of the City players had left their concentration in their lockers. The Sky Blues were caught offside eighteen times, Reading once, and presented their opponents with clear-cut chances from as early as the third minute. Eight minutes after half-time, Regis missed a glorious chance to put his team in front. Four minutes later, Neil Smillie scored for Reading. Speedie equalised after 71 minutes but the Biscuitmen were not going to let go. In extra time, City had the better opportunities but fluffed them all.

It was now into uncharted waters, City's first penalty shoot-out. Brian Kilcline put away the first penalty; Steve Ogrizovic superbly saved Keith Curle's effort and Greg Downs added a second for City with a crisp strike. Then it all went wrong. Stuart Beavon made it 1-2, Sedgley saw his shot saved and Dean Horrix equalised at 2-2. David Smith volunteered to take the next one after one of his senior team-mates reportedly chickened out. He scored but then Jerry Williams levelled. Steve Francis beat out Bennett's effort so it was all down to Michael Gilkes. It was fitting that he should score the winner – he had played Bennett out of the game.

The time was nearly twenty-to-eleven. Reading went on to crush Luton 4-1 at Wembley.

SUTTON UNITED v. COVENTRY CITY

7 January 1989
Gander Green Lane
FA Cup Third Round
Sutton United 2 Coventry City 1

For Coventry City, the draw for the third round of the Cup can be a bit like a visit to the Reptile House at London Zoo. There they are, the most venomous snakes lined up in a row: cobras, mambas, rattlesnakes, taipans. On each window you can read a CV of their deadly achievements. Among them is a humbler but more common killer called the saw-scaled viper. Saw-scaled vipers are plentiful in certain parts of the world. Tread on one of these camouflaged, nondescript creatures when you are a long way from help and its venom will most surely kill.

The twenty, apparently nondescript teams – some of them non-League – that make their way from the undistinguished ranks of hundreds of others to join the First and Second Division sides in the third round are the camouflaged threats. On a Somerset slope in 1949, Sunderland trod on Yeovil Town, with mortal consequences. In Herefordshire in 1972, Ronnie Radford spat like a cobra at Newcastle. In 1986, Altrincham from cosy Cheshire won at Birmingham. And in 1989, Coventry City visited the gin-and-jaguar belt of Surrey to play Sutton United.

Gander Green Lane sounds picturesque and innocent enough, like somewhere you might find the Fat Controller residing. The football ground is not an oasis amid smoky stacks but a field nestling between homes pitted with bird baths and stained glass. At one time it was the Adult School Sports Ground. Sutton United belonged to the heyday of the Isthmian League and the FA Amateur Cup. Now they were a semi-pro outfit, holding their own – but not much more – in the GM Vauxhall Conference. Average attendances that season, up by a quarter to 857, were poor even by the standards of the Conference. Meanwhile, it was less than twenty months since Sutton's visitors had won the Cup. Aside from David Speedie and David Smith, they were the same Coventry players.

There was a bumper crowd of 8,000. The Sky Blues were quick to create a hail of chances. This would be a formality. But a year before on this ground, Sutton had held promotion-chasing Middlesbrough to a draw. It soon became clear that, despite all the pre-match talk about not underestimating the opposition, City were struggling to turn superior ability to tangible effect.

Three minutes before the interval, Sutton scored. Oggy failed to deal with a corner to the near-post and the flick-on was headed in by the unmarked Tony Rains. However, we remained blasé at half-time. The prospect of an appalling embarrassment was surely enough to chasten our heroes. When David Phillips was put through by Steve Sedgley for an equaliser 7 minutes after the break, there were few – even Sutton diehards– who believed that the pumping of adrenaline and fitter legs would not now see Coventry home. But 6 minutes later there was more atrocious marking on the edge of the box and Matthew Hanlan volleyed Sutton into the lead. Unease turned to discomfort, discomfort gradually to panic. Cyrille Regis missed a sitter and was replaced by Keith Houchen. Hard as Houchen tried, this was not a day for Roy of the Rovers – certainly not in a Coventry shirt. Sutton dug in and, with a little luck, fought off everything that an increasingly desperate Coventry could throw at them. The final whistle went. Sutton United had won a richly deserved and famous victory. They were applauded from all around the ground.

Such a terrible and almost unprecedented result needs to be put in perspective. Six-and-a-half weeks later, City beat the eventual champions, Arsenal, to go third in the League. Unfortunately, the

F.A. CUP 3rd ROUND 09019

SUTTON UNITED
v.
COVENTRY CITY

at the Borough Sportsground, Gander Green Lane, Sutton
on Saturday 7 January 1989. K.O. 2.00 p.m.
Admission to Ground **£5**
Sold subject to ground rules as displayed

Sutton United 2-1 Coventry City.

season fell away although the Sky Blues were never out of the top eight. There were some deeply satisfying results to compensate for that one dreadful day. The Aston Villa bogey was laid after fifty-one years but not at Villa Park where City could have sent Villa down on the last Saturday. City did the double over Norwich City, who finished fourth, and Manchester United. The Cup Final side was dismantling: Nick Pickering, Dave Bennett and Keith Houchen were gone by March. But it was an exceptional season for David Speedie, and Tony Dobson came through to establish himself at left-back.

As always after such a result, the papers the next day were full of stories of the butcher, the baker and the candlestick maker. The two goalscorers received the accolade of an appearance on *The Wogan Show*. It was a triumph for Barrie Williams, the popular Sutton manager. Williams was fond of quoting Shakespeare, Kipling and the Venerable Bede in his programme notes. On this occasion, 'Our Visitors' slunk away with their tails between their legs, pursued by the brickbats of their own supporters. It had indeed been the most shocking defeat but in the context of the whole season not that shocking. Coventry City went on to finish seventh in the League, a position they have only once bettered. Sutton, meanwhile, were stung 8-0 at Norwich in the fourth round.

Nottingham Forest v. Coventry City

11 February 1990
City Ground
Littlewoods Cup Semi-Final First Leg
Nottingham Forest 2 Coventry City 1

It was never a penalty and their winner should have been disallowed. In any case, Pearce was lucky to be on the field for more than three minutes. It was one of those days, and a Sunday afternoon in February that belonged to an old-fashioned winter with its gale-force wind, driving rain and bog-like pitch.

In September, the Sky Blues had beaten Grimsby in the Littlewoods Cup, having lost the first leg 3-1. There followed away wins at Q.P.R. and Manchester City, before Sunderland were thrashed 5-0 in a quarter-final replay at Highfield Road, thanks to four goals from Steve Livingstone.

City paid a club-record fee of £900,000 for Dundee United's Scotland international forward, Kevin Gallacher. Gallacher was the grandson of Celtic's 'Mighty Atom', Patsy Gallacher. There was something of the mighty atom about Kevin himself, bowed over the ball like a hamster treading its wheel. This was only his fourth game for Coventry and Stuart Pearce immediately tried to soften him up with a thuggish challenge worthy of more than its yellow card.

Ken Redfern gave a 37th minute penalty against Cyrille Regis for handball. The ball had actually struck Regis on the thigh but the referee pointed to the spot despite being on the blind side and without the linesman raising his flag. Millions witnessed it on television. Nigel Clough struck the penalty almost apologetically. It was low and straight and the ball caught Steve Ogrizovic's foot as the City 'keeper dived to his right. It was a cruel blow for the Sky Blues who had started the stronger.

City kept battling and were rewarded with an equaliser halfway through the second half. Thorvaldur Orlygsson headed a clearance straight to Tony Dobson who, in the absence of the suspended Speedie, had been included in City's midfield for his snappy tackling and running. Dobson took the ball on but miscued an attempted shot. The ball looked set to slither through to Steve Sutton in the Forest goal until Livingstone raced round the defence and lifted it into the net.

The 7,000-strong Sky Blue Army were up for it now but 7 minutes later Forest restored their lead. Brian Kilcline gave away a direct free-kick when he shoved Nigel Jemson. Pearce thundered a left-foot shot around the wall, via the underside of the bar, and into the far corner. Should the goal have stood? Steve Hodge had pushed City's man of the match, Michael Gynn, to open up a huge gap in the wall. Mr Redfern overlooked it. City could yet have equalised 5 minutes from time when Dobson's fierce drive was parried by Sutton; Pearce somehow scooped the ball over the bar.

The Sky Blues did not create enough clear-cut chances. For all Forest's good fortune and City's competence, it left you suspecting that Brian Clough's team would show sufficient nous and resilience at Highfield Road in a fortnight's time. Thus it proved. A 0-0 draw was enough. Forest went to Wembley and beat Oldham Athletic 1-0.

In the FA Cup, the Sky Blues had already suffered a calamitous exit at Northampton. The rain was so torrential that fag packets and pound notes were soaked in the inside pockets of City fans standing on the open terrace.

The season had started with continued promise and by 30 August, City were sitting on top of the First Division for the first time ever. But less than a minute into their next game – at the Den, which was pungent with the smell of fresh creosote – City were on their way to conceding the leadership to Millwall. Speedie had to take over in goal from the injured Oggy for the second half.

Brian Borrows.

David Phillips, Steve Sedgley and Graham Rodger had left the club. Goalscoring, surprisingly, was the main problem and John Sillett paid Glasgow Rangers £800,000 for Kevin Drinkell. It was City's record fee prior to the signing of Gallacher but Drinkell was to prove only a fitful success. Northampton had exposed a Coventry side in which midfield guile had been supplanted by a less intuitive and more formulaic approach. For all that, City then rallied. They beat Villa, crushed Forest in a revenge match at the City Ground and in mid-March were fourth in the table. But it was an illusion. The season withered with only one win in the last 10 games and bad home defeats by Sheffield Wednesday and Charlton who were both relegated. It was completed with a 6-1 thrashing by Champions Liverpool – City's worst ever home League defeat. At the end of the match, Sillett made a point of warmly applauding the Liverpool fans while appearing to ignore the City supporters. The ice was getting thinner.

City finished twelfth. When would we next come as close to a major final?

COVENTRY CITY v. NOTTINGHAM FOREST

28 November 1990
Highfield Road
Rumbelows League Cup Fourth Round
Coventry City 5 Nottingham Forest 4

My nervous companion, grown grey with half a century of watching Coventry, would writhe uncomfortably even at 2 goals up. 'I've seen it all before, I don't trust the City,' he'd say. At 3 up though, his frown would ease a little, and certainly at 4 up there was a guarded optimism that we might hang on for a draw – so long as we were into injury time. You might think therefore that this match would have induced the need for immediate attention from the First Aiders, a quick rolling-up of the sleeve and a 'Count down from ten, please sir.' Instead, the harbinger felt reassured by being able to brandish 'I told you so' like fortune-tellers their references at a funfair.

The FA Cup was to elude Brian Clough but his Nottingham Forest side had made the League Cup their own, winning it in both of the last two seasons. It was the third season running that they had met Coventry in the competition. Incredibly, within thirty-five minutes of the kick-off, the Sky Blues were winning 4-0.

Kevin Gallacher prodded the ball in from close range to open the scoring after fourteen minutes. A minute later, Cyrille Regis threaded a pass to the right wing where Gallacher, from the edge of the area, exquisitely chipped the ball over the head of the floundering Mark Crossley who was well off his line. Just before the half-hour, Steve Livingstone took advantage of confusion in the Forest defence to score a third with a left-foot shot into the far corner. Then, Gallacher completed his hat-trick when he latched on to a Peter Billing header and volleyed athletically through the legs of a defender on the line. It was all over. Or so everyone thought.

It is not often that you see a player from both sides scoring a first half hat-trick but it happened in this game. Nigel Clough emulated his first goal, a shot from the arc of the D, with a sweetly struck second from the corner of the area. He then scrambled a third when Oggy parried the ball into his path. Many Forest fans had made an early exit in their disgruntlement but the contest was now vibrantly alive. On 53 minutes, Forest were level with a fourth goal within the space of 17 minutes. Garry Parker's shot found its way through some indifferent defending and inside Oggy's near post. Forest were not going to surrender their 22-match unbeaten run in the competition without a fight. It was two-and-a-half years since they had last conceded five goals in a match. But a fifth came. It was like pinball in the penalty area before Regis' powerful shot was headed in by Livingstone. There was nearly a third of the match to run but it was as if the game itself had grown weary from the excitement. Despite the prompting of Hodge and an innocent-faced Roy Keane, Forest could climb no further. It was City's night.

It was also Terry Butcher's night. It was his first win as a manager. Two months later, City meekly lost their quarter-final 1-0 at home to Sheffield Wednesday. Butcher was injured and the £400,000 City paid Glasgow Rangers for him as a player looked somewhat inflated.

The dismissal of John Sillett had left a sour taste. The feeling was that the board had been trying to engineer a change. Sillett learnt of it from his sickbed. It was not a propitious end.

In the days before we became used to a South American presence in the British game, the inclusion of the Uruguay captain José Perdomo, who six months previously had scored the winner against England at Wembley, was an exotic curiosity. Perdomo, who was on loan from Genoa, passed the ball with effortless accuracy. During his 6 games, he looked a class above anyone on the field, so

Kevin Gallacher completes his hat-trick.

much so that his patent lack of match fitness served only to accentuate the fact. Sadly, Sillett was not able to make his signing permanent.

After Butcher arrived, he appointed his former teammate Mick Mills as his assistant and there were the normal comings and goings. David Speedie was signed by Liverpool for £675,000, having looked set to join Villa. Speedie had been fined in September as a result of a well-publicised spat with one of City's vice-presidents, his disciplinary record was appalling, and he had repeatedly asked for a move. It may be churlish to add, given outstanding performances such as his headed hat-trick against Middlesbrough, that his strike rate was only marginally superior to that of Keith Houchen.

Robert Rosario arrived from Norwich for £650,000 as the putative successor to Regis. Kenny Sansom, the former England left-back, was signed from Newcastle and Stewart Robson came on loan from West Ham in an effort to rebuild his injury-smitten career. Robson made an instant impact and City climbed to ninth in the table. More than anything, however, it was the 16 goals Kevin Gallacher scored as a result of his conversion into an out-and-out striker that enabled the Sky Blues to finish the season in the reasonable comfort of sixteenth place.

ASTON VILLA v. COVENTRY CITY

2 May 1992
Villa Park
Barclays League Division One
Aston Villa 2 Coventry City 0

	P	W	D	L	F	A	W	D	L	F	A	GD	P
18 Norwich City	41	8	6	7	29	28	3	6	11	18	34	-15	45
19 Coventry City	41	6	7	8	18	15	5	4	11	17	27	-7	44
20 Luton Town	41	10	7	4	25	17	0	5	15	12	52	-32	42
21 Notts County	41	6	5	9	22	28	3	5	13	16	33	-23	37
22 West Ham United	41	5	6	9	19	24	3	5	13	15	35	-25	35

Having made your way from the station across the pathway above the purposeful traffic a long way below, your eyes are greeted, if the season is right, by colourful, carefully manicured flower beds. The city centre stretches out ahead. You begin to catch sight of more and more sky blue scarves. The disappearance of the floodlight pylons may have removed the shrine from any horizon but there is always that keen sense of anticipation, of common purpose, of a task to be fulfilled. So it is in the other direction, especially if the destination is Villa Park. It is quite likely for Coventry supporters that if it is the last day of the season everything will depend on that journey, the outcome of that final game. The target has shrunk to one moment, one match. All the weaknesses and shortcomings of a disappointing season have been gathered up into one last concerted effort.

What was disconcerting about this last day compared to all the other ones was that the team never rose to the challenge, yet survived. It was an abject performance. But Don Howe was still able to inflect his Brummie tones with suitable relief on *Sports Report*.

Terry Butcher had given Cyrille Regis to Aston Villa on a free transfer at the end of the previous season. At thirty-four, the great man had lost his puff but Ron Atkinson recognised that those inimitable short bursts were not yet completely shot. City had been crushed 6-1 by the champions in the final game at Highbury. It was not just a valedictory afternoon to Cyrille. With the sale of Brian Kilcline to Oldham, the pieces of the Cup-winning team were becoming rarer by the year.

Trevor Peake, too, was on his way soon after the start of the new season. Along with Lloyd McGrath and Kenny Sansom, he was sent home after the three of them had been discovered imbibing in Troon forty-eight hours before a pre-season tournament in Kilmarnock. They were heavily fined, and transfer listed. Some observed that it was a case of the sledgehammer and the nut.

Peake's place was taken by a young Wigan defender, Peter Atherton. Stewart Robson's transfer from West Ham was made permanent. Robson's form in midfield was one of the few individual highlights of the season. Another signing was an eighteen-year-old Zimbabwean, first spotted by John Sillett when City were on tour in his country in 1990. Peter Ndlovu was one of the most naturally talented players ever to appear for Coventry. Ndlovu's two brothers also became professional players but, according to Peter, the best player in the family was actually his sister.

City made a reasonable start, thrashing Luton 5-0 at Highfield Road and inflicting Arsenal's first home defeat for eighteen months with an Ndlovu winner. Paul Furlong, bought from Enfield as cover for up front, also made an early impression.

Highfield Road, 1985.

On 9 November, concerns about the financial situation at the club crystallised with the resignation of the Cup Final chairman, John Poynton. Poynton was replaced by for a second spell by Peter Robins, who was backed by Bryan Richardson and London lawyer Michael Jepson. Within days of the coup, Butcher was forced to sack his assistant Mick Mills and reserve-team coach Brian Eastick. Mills was replaced by Don Howe, whose CV in the game was without peer. Terry Butcher's final weeks were ignominious. He was sent off at the end of a Zenith Data Systems Cup-tie against Aston Villa and announced his retirement from playing after a poor run of form. In January, Howe replaced Butcher as manager in a caretaker capacity. Robins attempted to renegotiate Butcher's contract to reflect the fact that he had retired as a player. The repurcussions rumbled on in the courts.

Dion Dublin's injury-time winner for Cambridge United put City out of the FA Cup. There were 4 goalless draws running, and a depressing decline. An Easter Monday defeat at Leeds, inspired by Strachan and McAllister, was followed one game from the end by City's first home win since November, by the only goal against West Ham.

And so, to Villa Park. The coefficient was the game at Meadow Lane between Notts County and Luton. Notts County, along with West Ham, were already relegated. Within 21 seconds, City fell behind – to a header from Cyrille Regis. It got worse with news of a Luton goal. As things stood, City now needed to win to stay up, which looked even less likely when Dwight Yorke scored a second for Villa after 36 minutes. City were laying the final brick themselves as they slipped into the bottom three for the first time that season. Events on the field lost their relevance. All that mattered now was that famous old Notts County, founder members of the League, should summon up sufficient self-respect to go out fighting and drag Luton down with them. Every Coventry supporter was saying a prayer. And, bless them, Notts responded. The unexpected hero was Rob Matthews, who had joined Notts from Loughborough University only five weeks before. His 2 goals sent his future club down. Meanwhile, one Villa player was celebrating that his goal had not helped send his old club down.

COVENTRY CITY v. LIVERPOOL

19 December 1992
Highfield Road
FA Premier League
Coventry City 5 Liverpool 1

August 1992 saw the arrival of the Premier League. It was one of those moments, like decimalisation in 1971, that did not immediately fulfil all the fanfare and fuss. Of course, there was the irritation of learning to call the Second Division, Division One, and so on. But there were no disguises. The new castle would become less and less accessible, the moat ever deeper and the slings and arrows increasingly feeble. There was no place at the tournament for Robin Hood. Never again would the likes of Ipswich Town and Burnley make a serious nuisance of themselves. That was the point of it.

Yet, this victory over Liverpool was a colossal endorsement of Coventry City's ability still to compete with the most powerful. Winning their first 3 matches put the Sky Blues on top of the table; winning 4 away games on the trot was a club record.

In May, within days of being sacked as manager of West Bromwich, Bobby Gould returned to Coventry to share the reins with Don Howe. Since his last term at Highfield Road, Gould had led Wimbledon to FA Cup success, and he exuded the same bright confidence as ever. Howe would retain responsibility for coaching and tactics but, in the event, Gould's appointment gave him the opportunity to quietly withdraw. He decided that the daily trip from Hertfordshire was too much, and stepped down. In his few months in charge, the side had confirmed the dourness and defensiveness often associated with Howe's teams and, during the 1991/92 season, scored only 35 goals.

One of the things that a section of supporters did not take kindly to was Howe's re-employment of goalkeeper Les Sealey, albeit on loan. Sealey had made his indifference to the club only too apparent on his departure in 1983. It cost a subsequent *Evening Telegraph* reporter his job after he reiterated the notion that Sealey had let a goal in on purpose against West Ham at the end of the 1982/83 season.

Gould appointed Phil Neal, who had just been sacked as manager of Bolton, as his assistant. He then set about using his expert knowledge of the lower divisions again to acquire John Williams from Swansea and a young Bradford City defender, Phil Babb. A year before, Williams had been a postman. He won the Rumbelows Sprint Challenge at Wembley and his speed and goals took early opponents by surprise.

Two players in particular indented themselves in fans' favours: Peter Ndlovu and Mick Quinn. The teenaged Zimbabwean moulded the ball to his instincts as he teased and bewitched one unfortunate defender after another. Quinn was fleet of foot but stout. As 'Sumo' plundered 10 goals in his first 6 games, opposition fans chanted: 'Who ate all the pies? Who ate all the pies? You fat bastard, you fat bastard, you ate all the pies!'

Memories were invoked of almost exactly nine years before when Gould's team had crushed Liverpool 4-0. There was no reason to anticipate a repeat even if the Reds were only one place above City in the table.

Jonathan Gould was given his debut in goal in place of the injured Steve Ogrizovic, and Phil Babb made only his second start, marking Ian Rush. Liverpool dominated the first half but it was City who took the lead in the 37th minute with a penalty from Brian Borrows. It was Borrows, still

Peter Ndlovu.

against the run of play, who scored again 10 minutes after half-time. He smashed the ball home from an indirect free-kick. The Sky Blues began to ooze genuine confidence. Lee Hurst and Lloyd McGrath dominated midfield and a four-man front line of Gallacher, Rosario, Quinn and Williams picked big holes in the opposition defence. Gallacher tapped in a third on the hour from a Rosario pass. Jamie Redknapp pulled a goal back shortly afterwards with a 25-yarder. It was his last contribution; he was sent off for felling Gallacher. A few minutes later, Quinn snapped up two more chances and City, who finished the match with their opponents on the run, completed a thrilling victory.

Financial stress was never far away during the season. Robert Rosario was sold to Nottingham Forest, followed by Kevin Gallacher to Blackburn. Roy Wegerle arrived as part of the Gallacher deal and a philanthropic supporter put his hand into his own pocket, it was rumoured, for the £250,000 required to make Quinn's transfer permanent.

The season tailed away disappointingly with the Sky Blues gaining only a single win in their last 11 matches. On the last day, a 3-1 lead was surrendered in injury time against Leeds. It cost City, who finished fifteenth, three places in the table and £250,000 in prize money.

Chairman Peter Robins had spoken before the start of the season about large new sums of money being made available, but they did not materialise. In the summer of 1993, Robins stood down for the second time and became chief executive. The new chairman, already a member of the board, was publishing entrepreneur and former Warwickshire cricketer, Bryan Richardson.

TOTTENHAM HOTSPUR v. COVENTRY CITY

9 May 1995
White Hart Lane
FA Carling Premiership
Tottenham Hotspur 1 Coventry City 3

	P	W	D	L	F	A	W	D	L	F	A	GD	P
13 Manchester City	41	8	7	5	35	25	4	6	11	16	36	-10	49
14 Sheffield Wednesday	41	6	7	7	22	25	6	5	10	23	31	-11	48
15 Aston Villa	41	6	9	6	27	24	5	5	10	23	31	-5	47
16 West Ham United	40	8	5	6	24	18	4	5	12	16	29	-7	46
17 Everton	40	8	9	4	31	23	2	7	10	12	28	-8	46
18 Coventry City	40	7	6	7	23	25	4	7	9	18	36	-20	46
19 Crystal Palace	40	6	6	9	16	23	5	6	8	15	20	-12	45
20 Norwich City	41	8	7	5	26	20	2	5	14	10	33	-17	42
21 Leicester City	41	5	6	10	28	37	1	4	15	15	41	-35	28
22 Ipswich Town	40	5	3	12	24	33	2	3	15	11	55	-53	27

Gordon Strachan, sprung like a clockwork mouse it seemed, gave one of the greatest individual performances ever seen in a Coventry City shirt to ensure the Sky Blues of survival at the end of Big Ron's first season in charge.

Phil Neal had been sacked in February and was readily replaced by Atkinson. Ron, one of football's most enthusiastic characters, who infected all around him with his bonhomie and self-confidence, restored the club to the headlines that had withered and been withering about it in recent years. A smart alec, metropolitan snootiness had grown up in the national press and Bryan Richardson's desire to appoint a personality such as Atkinson was born partly out of reaction to this.

The Sky Blues had kicked-off the previous season with mixed fortune at Highbury. City won with a Mick Quinn hat-trick but, after 10 minutes, Stewart Robson went off with a knee injury, fate insisting that his attempt to rebuild a ravaged career should be frustrated forever. Despite further good results, things began to turn sour for manager Bobby Gould, and by October 1993 he was announcing his resignation to Richardson in the gents after a 5-1 defeat at Loftus Road. There had been no hint of this at lunchtime when he appeared as a chirpy studio guest on *Football Focus*. As a local boy and with Coventry City so close to his heart, he may have looked into the crystal ball that afternoon and taken stock of the long struggle ahead and its inevitable outcome. He had been stung by insinuations of nepotism over the preference for his son Jonathan in goal. Maybe he was also influenced by the intentions of John Clarke. Clarke, who had recently left the Coventry board, had a little bit of brass but not enough to mount a takeover bid on his own. Gould's resignation was the opportunity he needed to attempt to draw together a consortium. Gould played on the Ian Wallace factor by suggesting that Babb and Ndlovu were about to be sold to balance the books. Television was at Highfield Road the following weekend for the Sheffield United game and Gould was one of the guests on the programme. At the end of the match, fans demonstrated in front of the cameras. 'I feel so humbled,' Gould informed us as he acknowledged them. It was a tacky gesture at the end of a distinguished association. Neal took over and the team went on to finish eleventh.

There were two other controversial incidents during 1993/94. Lee Hurst's promising career was ended as a result of an injury sustained on an assault course in pre-season training, and Wolves

'One of the finest performances of
wing play I have ever witnessed',
Ron Atkinson.

were quicker on the uptake in signing Chris Marsden, whose canny coaxing had transformed the City midfield during a loan spell from Huddersfield.

Phil Babb was eventually sold as expected, but for a British record fee for a defender of £3.75 million. The fact that Liverpool reportedly paid all the money up front was to enable Neal to give £2 million to Manchester United for Dion Dublin.

Injuries and bad luck were the undoing of Neal and his experienced assistant, Mick Brown. The Premiership was to be reduced at the end of the 1994/95 season to twenty clubs. With four teams due for the drop, the board had become itchy.

Big Ron's impact was immediate. Five thousand extra fans appeared from nowhere to see City defeat West Ham and Leicester at Highfield Road. Three draws followed. Then, courtesy of a Peter Ndlovu hat-trick – the first by a visiting player at Anfield in thirty-three years – the Sky Blues beat Liverpool 3-2. Atkinson bought his old midfield general, Kevin Richardson, from Aston Villa and left-back David Burrows from Everton.

The run ended at Leeds. Gordon Strachan arrived from Elland Road as player/assistant manager. The idea was that he should succeed Atkinson in two years time.

Three games from the end, City suffered bitter defeat, at bottom-of-the-table Ipswich. Other unhelpful results left the team a point above the relegation zone.

It was a warm evening. There were unexpected changes with John Filan making his City debut in goal. The decision to restore Julian Darby proved felicitous.

Time never stops, however masterful a player's technique, however stringent his attention to diet and fitness. Yet, on this particular evening, a great footballer gave his last great performance, and time held its breath. Here was a furious, flame-haired little man, playing from his heart, prompting, teasing, accelerating, covering every blade of grass as the sun gave way to floodlight. With darkness enveloping the ground, Gordon Strachan became ever more insistent. Whirring like a spinning top, this thirty-eight-year-old tore round Justin Edinburgh – thirteen years his junior. He was upended and Ndlovu scored from the spot. It was the decisive moment. A diving header by Ndlovu – from Strachan's cross – had already given City a half-time lead.

There was nothing superfluous in Strachan's play. His was a perfect balance, a bundle of conviction – deft and incisive. He could suddenly trim his sail and pitch a pass from out of the other eye. Thus, he crossed again and Dublin scored a third. Anderton pulled one back in the last ten minutes.

Crystal Palace's defeat at Leeds made City's last match against Everton a grateful irrelevance. At White Hart Lane, long after floodlight had receded into night, the blaze of one man's performance continued to shine.

Manchester United v. Coventry City

8 April 1996
Old Trafford
FA Carling Premiership
Manchester United 1 Coventry City 0

The significance of this match lies in its insignificance.

The ghastly injury sustained by David Busst rendered any other consideration of secondary importance. The circus of players – teeth bared at snapping lenses, shirts strewn with sponsors' logos – shuddered to a halt. Championships and relegation were as mere pots and pans as our most vulnerable fears lay exposed.

At first glance, the pictures appeared to be of a bent knee. On closer inspection, you realised that it was actually the tibia of the right leg snapped at a right-angle.

David Busst came late to professional football. He was born in Birmingham and worked for Britannic Assurance as a financial adviser, playing football part-time for Solihull Borough, Kings Heath and, for several years, Moor Green. Word had got around about his performances in the Beazer Homes League. There could be nobody better qualified to assess his abilities than the former England captain Terry Butcher, like Busst a centre half. Butcher was now the manager of Coventry and he invited Busst to Highfield Road for a trial. Busst played 2 reserve games, one of them against Manchester United at Old Trafford. Terry Butcher's days at Coventry were numbered but the trialist's signing was completed by Don Howe. It was 14 January 1992. David Busst's dearest wish, to become a professional footballer, had been fulfilled.

It was a year later, under Bobby Gould's management, that Busst made his League debut, at the age of twenty-six. He was a strong and determined player with striking blonde hair. He soon brought fitness and finesse to the raw talent admired by Butcher. Despite changes of management and having to undergo two hernia operations, Busst established himself in the Premiership, making 50 appearances:

> I have had five years involvement with a Premiership club and I have very happy memories. My dad has kept a scrapbook and videos of matches I played in. I have the jersey I wore on my debut for the club and I have pictures of all my goals. But most of all I have memories of all the friendships I made in football.

It was Easter Monday. Only 87 seconds of the game had passed when Busst collided with Denis Irwin at United's far post. The City captain, Dion Dublin, whose career at Manchester United had been seriously interrupted by a broken leg, held Busst's hand as he lay on the ground. The Coventry physiotherapist, George Dalton, was soon in attendance. Dalton himself had been forced to retire at twenty-seven after twice breaking a leg. In his first years as a qualified physio with Birmingham City, he had saved the career of the fledgling Trevor Francis. In that case, there was a hidden injury, a snapped tendon behind the knee and while even specialists had differed on the need for surgery or rest, it was Dalton's perseverance that ensured that Francis would not be risked until surgical exploration had been carried out.

There were two doctors on the pitch, but, as Dalton said: 'Normally it comes down to the physio. The job was to get Davo onto the stretcher without twisting him.' Dalton then had to make judgements in a matter of seconds that would have taxed an orthopaedic specialist as he organised the lifting of Busst on to the stretcher, combining speed and compassion, before the ambulance

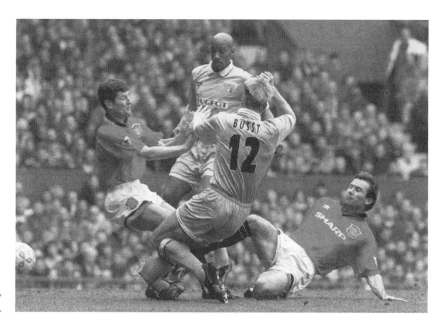

Old Trafford,
8 April, 1996.

men took over. Once he was in the hands of Raymond Ross, the orthopaedic consultant, the full extent of the damage to Busst's leg, which was more consistent with a motorcycle accident than a sporting injury, became clear.

The game was held up for nearly nine minutes. Sand was shovelled onto the pitch. Peter Schmeichel, the Manchester United goalkeeper, was so distressed that he needed to be comforted later by a doctor.

In 1987, after being transferred to Tottenham, Danny Thomas had his career wrecked as a result of a disgraceful challenge by Gavin Maguire of Q.P.R. In 2000, a shocking tackle by Nicky Summerbee of Sunderland ended Steve Froggat's career and the player's dreams of winning a first England cap a few days later. However, what happened at Old Trafford was no more than fateful. Such a freakish and very public accident shocked and touched the nation as well as everyone connected with the two football clubs. Among thousands of messages of good will was one from the Prime Minister.

David Busst had fifteen operations. His playing career was finished. On 16 May 1997, Manchester United came to Highfield Road to play a Coventry City Select XI in a benefit match. The place was packed to the rafters. Paul Gascoigne, as aware as most of the trauma of serious injury, was one of the guests in the City team. Alex Ferguson had this to say in the programme:

> None of us will forget David's horrendous injury and we didn't need any pressing to accept the invitation to come to Highfield Road. Courage comes in many forms and David has shown a particularly brave attitude facing up to the innumerable operations he has undergone... we all send him our best wishes for the future in the knowledge that his character is such that I'm sure he will still make his mark on life.

David Busst, with echoes of Tennyson, commented: 'It is better to have done it for only 5 minutes, than not at all.'

COVENTRY CITY v. LEEDS UNITED

5 May 1996
Highfield Road
FA Carling Premiership
Coventry City 0 Leeds United 0

	P	W	D	L	F	A	W	D	L	F	A	GD	P
14 Wimbledon	37	5	6	8	27	33	5	4	9	28	37	-15	40
15 Sheffield Wednesday	37	7	5	7	30	31	3	4	11	17	29	-13	39
16 Coventry City	37	6	6	6	21	23	2	7	10	21	37	-18	37
17 Southampton	37	7	6	5	21	18	2	4	13	13	34	-18	37
18 Manchester City	37	7	6	5	19	17	2	4	13	12	39	-25	37
19 Queens Park Rangers	37	6	5	8	25	26	3	1	14	13	28	-16	33
20 Bolton Wanderers	37	5	4	10	16	31	3	1	14	22	38	-31	29

The Unconventional Minister was the title Geoffrey Robinson gave to an account, published in 2000, of his life inside New Labour. The former chief executive of Jaguar was elected MP for Coventry North West in 1976. In his book, Robinson describes how he had resolved, on the day after Coventry City won the FA Cup, that if TransTec – his small high-tech company – was a success, and if he had the capital to spare, he 'would put it into the club to secure it a position amongst the top half-dozen teams in the country'. On his appointment as Paymaster General in Tony Blair's government, he resigned his directorship of the club and accepted an invitation to become President.

Robinson had met Bryan Richardson for lunch at the Grosvenor House in November 1995. The plan was simple, although Robinson stressed that the decision would not be his but the trustees of his 'family trust'. There could be up to £10 million invested in the club: £5 million straight away and a further £5 million during the season. Robinson suggested that Richardson try to secure a sizeable block of shares for the trust as part of the deal and invite him to join the board and become joint deputy chairman with Mike McGinnity. 'Thus began a period of quite remarkably productive co-operation between Bryan Richardson and myself. He and I have never had cross words', wrote Robinson. Derek Higgs, a highly respected City figure, accepted an invitation to join the board in 1997. Along with Richardson and Robinson, Higgs felt that a recapitalisation of the club was required to put it on a firmer financial footing. Serious negotiations were conducted with several financial organisations but they came to nothing. 'However, one avenue of development turned out to be a real winner. This was the building of a new stadium'. There has been a lot of water that has since flowed under the bridge.

The initial purchase with the trust loan was Noel Whelan who cost £2 million from Leeds. At first sight, Whelan appeared brittle but his was an exceptional, subtle, and highly coveted talent.

Big Ron's first full season started with bullish optimism but without Steve Bull, the Wolves striker, who decided to stay at Molineux. Nevertheless, there was plenty of summer transfer activity, although some of the signings were of a distinctly speculative nature. Of the major newcomers, Paul Telfer and Paul Williams played significant roles, although John Salako was never quite to fulfil the extraordinary talent that had earned him England recognition prior to a serious injury. Would the new signings really address the weaknesses in the team?

The Sky Blues plunged deep down the table during a wretched autumn but came from 2 goals down to beat Tottenham in the Coca-Cola Cup. A spate of red cards undermined attempts to

Coventry City v. Leeds United, 5 May 1996.
The last match before the demolition of the Spion Kop (*right*) and the removal of the floodlight pylons.

consolidate form in the League, although a hat-trick from Dublin helped the Sky Blues to thrash Champions Blackburn 5-0 on a snowbound Highfield Road pitch early in December.

Richard Shaw arrived from Crystal Palace for £1 million and further 7-figure deals for central defender Liam Daish and the skilful Scotland forward Eoin Jess brought Atkinson's spending, with and without the help of the trust, to over £13 million. A good Christmas sent the team into New Year with renewed zest but, by mid-March, a home defeat by bottom-of-the-table Bolton bore the tease of catastrophe.

Whelan's winner against Liverpool signalled the start of a recovery. Six thousand City fans took over the Arthur Wait Stand at Selhurst Park at the penultimate match against Wimbledon and saw Peter Ndlovu keep his composure to score both goals and inspire the Sky Blues to victory.

Eyebrows had been raised when Manchester United bought Dion Dublin from Cambridge United, a functional side of few frills. However, Dublin refined his skills and, later at Coventry, developed into one of the best target men in the business. He revealed his versatility at Selhurst Park by playing a commanding role as a makeshift centre-back.

Once again it had come down to the line. A goalless draw against Leeds proved to be enough but not before the usual ritual of distress had been fully drawn out. All seemed rosy with Manchester City 2 down against Liverpool but they pulled back to 2-2. Late in the game, the Maine Road crowd picked up on the erroneous information that one of the other clubs in trouble was losing. Alan Ball communicated this to his team who concentrated on just keeping possession. It must have been a painful lesson in the integrity of rumour. With Southampton drawing 0-0 at home to Wimbledon, Manchester City were the ones to be relegated.

Richardson and Atkinson had succeeded, with Robinson's help, in altering the image of the club. There was a steep increase in attendances. Gary McAllister was on his way. Surely, the breakthrough was just around the corner.

TOTTENHAM HOTSPUR v. COVENTRY CITY

11 May 1997
FA Carling Premiership
White Hart Lane
Tottenham Hotspur 1 Coventry City 2

	P	W	D	L	F	A	W	D	L	F	A	GD	P
16 Southampton	37	6	7	6	32	24	4	4	10	18	31	-5	41
17 Sunderland	37	7	6	6	20	18	3	4	11	15	34	-17	40
18 Middlesbrough	37	8	5	6	34	25	2	6	10	16	34	-9	38 *
19 Coventry City	37	4	8	7	19	23	4	6	8	17	30	-17	38
20 Nottingham Forest	37	3	9	7	15	27	3	7	8	16	27	-23	34

* Middlesbrough deducted 3 points

Little did we know it but Lady Luck was lavishing her largesse on City for the last time. This was to be the most outrageous of last-day escapes.

How unlikely it all looked eight days before. Home defeat by Derby and wins for Middlesbrough and Sunderland had dropped City into the relegation zone. The execution breakfast was the only thing to look forward to. On Monday, Middlesbrough – docked 3 points early in the season – drew with the champions elect at Old Trafford. They picked up another point at Blackburn on Thursday. So long as we won at Tottenham – oh, and so long as Middlesbrough and Sunderland didn't win – we'd be saved.

Sunderland supporters, with memories of 1977, were quick to spot a conspiracy when the kick-off at White Hart Lane was delayed until 4.15p.m. because of problems on the M1. Certainly, if all was going well it might make the last 15 minutes less frantic for the Sky Blues. Despair had turned to childlike optimism as the week wore on. It really was possible: we could do it.

Gary McAllister became the highest profile signing in Coventry City's history. He was a lean figure with an expression neither angular nor avuncular, a playmaker casting his fly as fastidiously as a fisherman from the riverbank. Despite the confidence generated by McAllister's arrival, a 7-1 pre-season thrashing by Benfica and a 3-0 home defeat by Nottingham Forest quickly sowed apprehension.

There were farcical scenes at Stamford Bridge in the third game of the season when the officials seemed to be the only people in the ground to miss a flagrant handball by Petrescu; Chelsea's first goal was allowed to stand. Liam Daish was sent off for registering his dissatisfaction and Ron Atkinson and Gordon Strachan were heavily fined for 'bringing the game into disrepute' with their subsequent comments.

By 4 November, City had managed just 4 goals in 11 League games and were nineteenth. There was murmuring from behind the scenes and an earlier than agreed handing over to Gordon Strachan. Atkinson caustically commented that he would not be voting Labour again, Geoffrey Robinson being perceived as the instigator of a press leak.

When Strachan took the reins, he appointed Alex Miller as his assistant. Miller was Craig Brown's number two as Scotland manager and a peer to whom Strachan felt disposed to respond.

Big Ron had signed Darren Huckerby from Newcastle just before the changeover, Kevin Keegan having decided to disband Newcastle's reserve team. Huckerby scored on his home debut – against

Steve Ogrizovic
and Paul Williams.

Newcastle – as Strachan began to take a grip. Strachan's biggest early signing was Gary Breen, who cost £2.5 million from Birmingham City. Breen was a stylish central defender but his relationship with his new manager was to grow sour.

The team spent the rest of term anxiously playing catch-up after the bad start. The high spot of a disappointing season was winning in the 92nd minute at Anfield.

Come the last day at White Hart Lane, 4,200 City fans behind Oggy's goal erupted as Dublin headed in McAllister's cross to give the Sky Blues a 12th-minute lead. Four City players were booked by Martin Bodenham for fouls within the first 24 minutes. Too much was at stake. Noel Whelan hobbled off to be replaced by Eoin Jess. When Paul Williams caressed a volley into the net from the edge of the area to double the lead after 38 minutes, the summery swathe of sky blue became volcanic.

Rumour and counter-rumour swept neurotically across the terrace; half-heard news from radios teasingly broke and receded across the shore. There was no score in the other 2 matches which had reached half-time. It was going OK, we were right to have had hope.

However, within 5 minutes, fate entered a word of caution. Dublin was pulled up for a foul just outside the area. Teddy Sheringham curled the free-kick over the wall. The ball thudded against a post and fell kindly for Paul McVeigh to score. It was half-time.

Leeds scored in the 77th minute at Elland Road. Juninho equalised 2 minutes later but Middlesbrough could not force a winner. At Selhurst Park, Sunderland went down to a Wimbledon goal in the last 5 minutes. Suddenly, it was all up to us. There were 15 minutes to go. We had been not waving but drowning; now, we could see the sand beneath our feet. As the sea got shallower, the water began to match the blue of the sky.

Oggy, the ex-copper with a nose as crooked as a flash of lightning, pulled off two stupendous saves. We were into time added on. Unexpectedly, Mr Bodenham blew his whistle after only a few seconds. It was all over.

Gary McAllister wiped away tears of relief and declared: 'This is the greatest achievement of my career.' 'This is a fabulous day,' he said,

When I came here in the summer, I was the main man – the £3 million signing who was supposed to make things happen. I am the captain of the team and feel responsible. We have had a poor season, we all know that, but to win like this is terrific. I came here because I thought that Coventry City were going to go places, everybody thought that. It has not happened this season but because of today it can.

LIVERPOOL v. COVENTRY CITY

3 January 1998
Anfield
FA Cup Third Round
Liverpool 1 Coventry City 3

Scouse humour tends to favour the laconic above the reassuring. Hence, with what appeared to be a tornado swirling across the Mersey and the taxi being buffeted from side to side, our driver's sense of comedy was delightfully inappropriate. Meanwhile, inside the ground, a Coventry fan was spouting invective, his lower lip smarting with regularity from the sixth letter of the alphabet. Suddenly, part of his upper set shot out. Amidst the merriment, someone gingerly recovered his device from two rows in front. The fact that the owner subsequently moderated his language owed less perhaps to an enlightenment of discretion than to Coventry City's outstanding performance.

After the narrow escape of the previous May, Gordon Strachan was beginning to build a Coventry team of verve and aplomb. There were some important newcomers. One of these was Roland Nilsson. Big Ron's last act before resigning the largely superfluous position as Director of Football was to facilitate his transfer. Nilsson cost £200,000 and a young midfielder from Feyenoord, George Boateng, not much more. In December, Magnus Hedman displaced Oggy and by the end of the year Viorel Moldovan was signed from Grasshoppers for a club record fee of £3.25 million.

Nilsson had the look of a dapper lunch guest about him, happy to have a kick-around with the kids before the consommé whilst insouciantly disdaining thought of any possible threat to his clothes or coiffure. From his home in Helsingborg, he could look across the Baltic's narrowest aperture to the castle of Elsinore, a prince among players.

At first sight, Boateng resembled Lloyd McGrath but he strutted rather than shuffled and there was more to his game than mere teeth, as he showed at Anfield. With the full implications of the Bosman ruling yet to take effect in the United Kingdom, Coventry became one of the first clubs to appoint a European scout. Ray Clarke's brief was to recommend talent, both proven and prospective, that could save the club money in the British transfer market. Boateng was one of Clarke's most noteworthy coups. With a serious knee injury bringing McAllister's season – and World Cup aspirations – to a premature end, Boateng's arrival could not have been more timely.

McAllister's injury came a few weeks after a win against Newcastle which saw Dion Dublin score the most bizarre of goals. Shay Given, the visiting 'keeper, grasped the ball from Dublin's head and placed it on the ground. The momentum had carried Dublin behind the goal-line and he appeared to take time for a chat with the customers before re-entering the fray, rounding the unsuspecting Given and flicking the ball into the net.

Moldovan was to have City fans jumping to their feet when he scored for Romania against England in the World Cup that summer. His impact at Coventry was immediate but vicarious: Dublin and Huckerby suddenly woke up.

At Highfield Road on the Sunday before the Liverpool game, the Sky Blues had beaten Manchester United 3-2 in a sensational climax to the game. City, who had scored first through Noel Whelan, fell behind to goals from Solskjaer and Sheringham. Four minutes from time, Dublin equalised from the spot. And then with 2 minutes left, Huckerby took off on a mazy run, got his head down oblivious to anything but the slalom ahead of him, and scored a wonderful winner.

Right: Dion Dublin, Coventry City and England.

Far right: Darren Huckerby.

Liverpool were ahead at Anfield after seven minutes, Jamie Redknapp scoring with a free-kick. With the first half running out, Huckerby twisted and turned on the left-hand side of the Liverpool area, dribbled past three defenders and planted the ball beyond David James. It was a magnificent goal and similar to his one against Manchester United. Dublin put City ahead just after the hour when James parried a shot from Huckerby who had again got through the defence. The Sky Blues were dominating the game. With only 3 minutes to go they scored a third. Dublin again put Huckerby through. Huck's shot rattled off the far post for Paul Telfer to bury the ball; James was stranded. It had been a devastating performance by Huckerby but it was the industry of Boateng and Whelan that had made things possible.

City knocked out Derby at Highfield Road in the next round. It was Villa Park then for Round Five where, midway through the second half, a pass from Strachan's son, Gavin, found Boateng. Boateng skipped past three players. Bosnich parried his shot but Villa had no time to flash their cross as the Transylvanian Moldovan bared his teeth and buried the chance. It was City's first win at Villa Park, at the twenty-seventh attempt.

A quarter-final at home to Sheffield United looked less of a challenge. The Blades had done their homework though, and City never looked likely to add to Dublin's penalty once their opponents had equalised. In the final minutes, Ogrizovic, back in the side because of injury to Hedman, ran 30 yards from his line to clear the ball. He hit it straight at a Sheffield United player. The crowd held its breath. Oggy must have gasped at his years and all the cigarettes he may have puffed. Fortunately, his desperate recovery sent the ball skimming to safety off the post.

The replay itches the memory in a series of snapshots: Telfer's early goal, Moldovan's missed chance, an inevitable equaliser that sadistically arrived in the last minute, the hopelessness of extra time and the penalty shoot-out that unravelled itself at the end of a late evening a long way from home.

If that evening was a story of lost opportunity, the season as a whole was one of achievement. In the New Year, City hit a 13-match unbeaten run, which included 7 wins on the trot. Dublin, who was joint top-scorer in the Premiership with 18 goals, played for England and Huckerby, who scored 14, for England 'B'.

The gentleman with the false teeth would not be the only one to reflect. Coventry had beaten both Manchester United and Liverpool in the space of a few days. This was more than fortune cocking a wink at a plucky effort. The quality of the second-half performance at Anfield suggested that Coventry City could compete with the very best. Bryan Richardson and Gordon Strachan were seeing their fruits begin to ripen.

Aston Villa v. Coventry City

27 February 1999
Villa Park
FA Carling Premiership
Aston Villa 1 Coventry Ciy 4

'Shit on the Villa tonight,' chant Coventry City supporters. You probably need to be a Coventrian to really get the Villa thing. It is a bit like the Scottish obsession with beating England. How did it all start? Is it a throwback to the games in the 1930s? Is it perhaps about Coventry living in the shadow of England's second city? Whatever the case, this was Coventry's Bannockburn. After the Cup win the year before, it was City's first victory in 25 league visits to Villa Park.

Aston Villa lost their First Division place for the first time in 1936. At the end of the same season, Coventry City were promoted from the Third Division. The interest and excitement generated over the next two years by the clubs' rivalry was intense. When the fixtures were released in that year of Abdication and Spanish Civil War, all local eyes were on the dates of the Villa games. When Villa admitted the Bantams to their coop for the first time on 3 October, 15,000 people made the trip from Coventry. The crowd of 63,686 watched a 0-0 draw. There were 39,808 at Highfield Road for the return on 6 February, City's Jackie Brown scoring the only goal of the game. At Villa Park the following October, the attendance was 68,029, including about 20,000 from Coventry. The game finished 1-1 with Bill McDonald scoring first for the Bantams. By the time 44,930 crammed into Highfield Road in March, the two teams were battling for promotion. Villa won 1-0 and went on to win the Second Division Championship. That was the end of League fixtures between the two clubs until 1975, but City lost at Villa Park in the FA Cup in 1946 and 1965.

The close season of 1998 confirmed Bryan Richardson as an astute dealer in the transfer market. Viorel Moldovan signed for Fenerbahce after only half-a-season at Highfield Road, netting City a £750,000 profit. Then, Robert Jarni – one of Croatia's World Cup heroes, had second thoughts about coming to Coventry and was sold on to Real Madrid for a £735,000 profit before he had even entered the dressing room, let alone laced up his boots.

The big question was over the future of Dion Dublin. Coventry anticipated Dublin's career stretching ahead with the player's ability to fall back and play as a central defender. With only a year left on his contract, the club agreed a £1 million per annum deal. This failed to put the lid on matters though, as Dublin had a clause in his contract allowing him to talk to any club prepared to offer City more than £5 million for his services. Coventry accepted Blackburn's offer of £6.75 million but were forced to accept £5.75 million from Aston Villa, Dublin having preferred their terms. The relationship between Coventry and Villa became extremely strained and was exacerbated by the circumstances later of George Boateng's transfer. Richardson alleged that Villa made an illegal approach for Boateng.

The two most expensive newcomers of the season were Stephen Froggatt, the Wolves winger, and Muhamed Konjic, Monaco's Bosnia international centre-back. Froggatt had been signed to provide the service for Dublin but they only played 3 games together before Dublin's departure. Froggatt's career was destroyed by injury a year later and Konjic's injury problems soon put him out of favour with Gordon Strachan who was loth to select him even when fit.

The Dublin saga undermined team spirit. Morale was further punctured by a reported dressing-room row before the fifth round Cup-tie at Everton, which was to prompt one of City's most listless performances.

Bryan Richardson.

The Australian striker John Aloisi arrived after another smart piece of negotiation. He was to have an important impact when City, uncomfortably close to the relegation zone, ran out at Villa Park. His approach play was rarely auspicious but it focussed as the penalty area began to shrink.

It was clear when Dublin emerged from the tunnel that he had forfeited the esteem in which Coventry supporters had always held a previous Villa exile, Cyrille Regis. The first 20 minutes were 'even Stevens'. However, after 24 minutes, City scored. Aloisi brought Froggatt's cross under control, pushed the ball past Riccardo Scimeca and slid his shot diagonally beyond the outstretched goalkeeper, Michael Oakes. Paul Williams was booked for pulling Julian Joachim's shirt on the edge of the box. There was a second Villa substitution when Steve Watson was carried off shortly before half-time.

Boateng was playing a blinder in midfield, which was probably what led John Gregory to covet his services. He scored a marvellous goal five minutes after the break. Darren Huckerby escaped from Gareth Southgate on the right and fed the ball to the near post where Boateng turned and lifted it over Scimeca and Oakes into the roof of the net. Within minutes, Villa pulled one back after Richard Shaw had been adjudged to have brought down Joachim. The scorer – needless to say – was Dublin. He struck the ball to Magnus Hedman's left in a departure from his routine at Coventry. Villa stepped up the pressure for an equaliser but, after 72 minutes, the Sky Blues again extended their lead. Froggatt's free-kick into the six-yard box was met first time by Aloisi. Huckerby created two further chances before City put it beyond Villa's reach, Boateng springing the offside trap and lobbing the ball over Oakes' head.

Dublin got booked, sixteen-year-old Gary McSheffrey came on as sub, the whistle blew and the Sky Blue Army went into rapture.

Aloisi was sent off the following weekend when City came from behind to beat Charlton with a well-controlled goal by Trond Soltvedt. Against Middlesbrough, Strachan appeared unprepared to send on his untried substitute goalkeeper, Chris Kirkland, when Hedman was injured early in the match. Safety was secured in the penultimate game. The season had been a disappointment.

Roland Nilsson fractured two ribs and punctured a lung in a freak incident at Arsenal in March. He recovered to make an emotional farewell in the last game. We did not know that it was only to be *au revoir*.

COVENTRY CITY v. ARSENAL

26 December 1999
Highfield Road
FA Carling Premiership
Coventry City 3 Arsenal 2

The Moroccans gave the lie to the suggestion that foreign imports are mere dilettantes and mercenaries beside their honest Tommy teammates. Gordon Strachan was so enamoured with Chippo and Hadji that despite the need to negotiate the constraints of Ramadan and the African Nations Cup he would happily have signed the whole national side. He later went back for Youssef Safri. Meanwhile, many a fan could be seen emerging from the club shop festooned in a fez.

Not everyone is a Moroccan. Bryan Richardson agreed with Strachan that the Belgium right-back Régis Genaux was the worst person they had ever known. The club cast their net as wide as Central America and as far south as the Andes. The relative failure of Zuniga, Guerrero and Martinez may have owed as much to the club underestimating the need to ingratiate the youngsters in their new surroundings as to any shortcomings in ability and potential.

As Mo Konjic strode forward like a soldier from the trench, the inimitable chant went up: 'He comes from Bos-ni-a, he is a big fu-cker.' Few Coventry players endeared themselves as much as Konjic over the coming seasons.

Youssef Chippo was signed from Porto for £1 million after City's inadequate campaign in 1998/99. Moustapha Hadji, African Player of the Year and Chippo's better-known compatriot in this new armada, landed from La Coruña in a £4 million transfer from Deportivo. The two of them brought more than ponytails and a cosmopolitan background. Their lithe style and languid skills were to contribute a more malleable dimension to City's attack. Amid unpleasant publicity, George Boateng finally went to Aston Villa for £4.5 million but as fans arrived at Filbert Street for the second game of the season to the news of Darren Huckerby's £5.5 million transfer to Leeds, the urgent requirement was a goalscorer.

Alex Ferguson had publicly turned his nose up at a young Irishman; other clubs had been tempted but had not had the courage, wondering whether the teenager could make the step up to the Premiership. Strachan expressed his admiration and Richardson moved heaven and earth and £6 million to sign him. Rarely has a player had such an immediate and sensational impact on Coventry City as Robbie Keane. Keane set off on a coruscating run, scoring from the narrowest of angles and adding a second on his Highfield Road debut against Derby. Never had a moment been so right, confidence in a teenage talent so utterly vindicated, as Robbie Keane cart-wheeled into our hearts.

There were two other newcomers who were fundamental to the shaping of the team: Carlton Palmer and Cedric Roussel. The experienced Palmer gave physical support to a midfield shorn of Boateng, and Roussel, a young centre forward from Belgium, provided a fulcrum to the attack.

Paul Telfer and Steve Froggatt played as full-backs in a very attacking team. Against Arsenal, it was Telfer's cross that enabled Gary McAllister to open the scoring after 25 minutes. McAllister's shot from way outside the box deflected off Martin Keown. Hadji – no whirling dervish, more a fencer – was at the heart of everything and put City further ahead a few minutes before half-time. Receiving the ball from McAllister on the edge of the box, he hoisted a shot above Adams and Keown which found the only exposed part of David Seaman's goal, just inside the right-hand post.

There were chances at both ends in an eventful first half and Hedman made good saves from Overmars, Petit and Henry.

Arsenal came more into the game after the break. Ljungberg, fed by Kanu, scored after 67 minutes but it was a scrappy goal for the City backline to concede. The Sky Blues soon restored their two-goal advantage with an astonishing goal by Keane. Paul Williams' free-kick was headed into the box by Palmer for Roussel to flick on. Keane was running away from the goal with Tony Adams at his heels. He caught the ball on the outside of his right foot and flicked it back past Seaman into the far corner of the net. It was a fitting climax to a wonderful individual performance. Suker scored for Arsenal in the dying minutes but this Coventry team was well up to hanging-on. It had been a display of great style and one to delight all City supporters.

On the morning of the return match in March, Magnus Hedman was passed unfit and missed his first game for fifteen months. Steve Ogrizovic, aged forty-two, stepped in for his 599th first-team game for City. Oggy had undergone surgery on a severe neck injury since his last appearance but at Highbury he was leaping around as enthusiastically as a boy on a beach. His performance prevented Arsenal from winning by a rugby score.

It may seem strange to recall with satisfaction a season in which the club had the worst away record in its history – 7 points, 9 goals and not a single win; odd to reflect that, for a time, European qualification looked feasible. It was all very different at home where the quality of televised performances earned City the sobriquet of 'The Entertainers'. Only Manchester United and Arsenal won more home matches. Even a defeat by Charlton in the fifth round of the Cup could not detract from the pleasure of watching football of the highest quality ever consistently played at Highfield Road.

Robbie Keane.

Aston Villa v. Coventry City

5 May 2001
Villa Park
FA Carling Premiership
Aston Villa 3 Coventry City 2

	P	W	D	L	F	A	W	D	L	F	A	GD	P
15 West Ham United	36	5	6	7	21	20	4	6	8	20	28	-7	39
16 Middlesbrough	36	3	7	8	16	22	5	7	6	25	20	-1	38
17 Derby County	36	8	6	4	22	23	1	5	12	13	35	-23	38
18 Manchester City	36	4	3	11	19	29	4	7	7	20	32	-22	34
19 Coventry City	36	4	6	8	14	23	4	3	11	20	37	-26	33
20 Bradford City	35	4	6	8	19	28	1	3	13	9	35	-35	24

And so, after all these years, a fantastic effort has failed. At the end of winter when afternoons return, the Sky Blues tottered and fell. It had been coming all season. Finally, it was merely eleven men sloping sadly from a football field. But, to Sky Blues supporters on the ground, fixed fast in a profound defeat, and to so many people in Coventry, it was a grievous blow to pride and self respect.

Coventry City's ability to hang on among the elite of English football became the regular butt of ill-informed sarcasm. So often had the parachute failed to open, it seemed, only for the angels to grasp us at the last possible moment. We were rarely very close to the sun but, like Icarus, we were bound one day to lose our wings.

Survival though is not really about getting lucky on the last day. Coventry City's average end-of-season position placed the club among the top fifteen in English football through three-and-a-half decades. That is a staggering achievement and could not have come about without a lot of good players, playing a lot of good football.

Those who scorn the narrow escapes during those 34 seasons should reflect on the forty-six clubs that failed to escape. They include: Manchester United, Tottenham, Chelsea, Leeds, Newcastle and, yes, Aston Villa. While Crystal Palace, Leicester and Sunderland experienced relegation from the top flight five times during this period, only Arsenal, Everton and Liverpool avoided it.

How ironic that this fateful game should be played out at Villa Park, but how optimistically it all began. Playing towards the Holt End against a Villa side containing Dion Dublin and George Boateng, the Sky Blues opened up a two-goal lead within the first 25 minutes.

Gareth Barry misdirected a routine pass to the feet of John Eustace. Eustace raced upfield and slipped the ball wide to Paul Telfer on the right, who prodded it forward a touch before curling an early cross into the box. Moustapha Hadji hurled himself at the ball and headed past David James to open the scoring. Seventeen minutes had gone.

Eustace was lucky to get away with a stern talking-to when he threw himself feet first into a full bloodied challenge that grounded Darius Vassell. Moments later, Hadji doubled City's lead with a real captain's effort. Racing on to a clearance from Paul Williams over the top of Villa's back four, the Moroccan darted between Southgate and Barry. He took one touch to take the ball into the area and then, as if with elastic in his boot, flashed a left-footed, angled volley past James into the far corner. It was a moment of rare bravura in a wretched season for City. With the exhileration of it, Hadji then tried to catch the 'keeper off his line with a long shot from the edge of the centre

Right: Moustapha Hadji.

Far right: Gordon Strachan.

circle.

An accidental injury to Telfer, who fractured his left leg, proved to be the turning-point of the game. Only noticed by some punters when he made a mistake, Telfer was a player's player, an integral well-oiled cog in the machine. He had been making even more impact in the middle than in his normal flanking role despite playing with a fractured cheek bone for three games.

The news from Valley Parade at half-time was more encouraging than from Old Trafford. It looked more ominous as Villa, inspired by substitute David Ginola, woke up. In the 61st minute, Delaney took the ball to the byline and crossed to the near post where a mix-up between Paul Williams and Chris Kirkland resulted in the goalkeeper fumbling the ball into the path of Vassell, who finished from close range. The emergence of Kirkland had been one of the few compensations of the season.

The ceiling collapsed on City in the last 10 minutes. Firstly, Juan Pablo Angel – Villa's under-achieving £9.5 million pound signing from River Plate – replaced Vassell and scored his first Villa goal. Then, with five minutes remaining, a spectacular long-range shot from Paul Merson put things beyond all hope. The roar of the opposition fans was as lonely an experience for Sky Blues followers as any in those thirty-four years. We were gone.

As the tumbrel swept City to oblivion, we could console ourselves that Villa's victory was superfluous. Manchester United, who put out virtually a reserve team in losing to Derby, and Middlesbrough, who took a point at Bradford City, ensured that the Sky Blues would have been relegated whatever the result at Villa Park.

Someone held up a makeshift placard. We'll Be Back was the defiant declaration. We walked past Aston church knowing that it was going to take more than faith for it to be possible.

We had not been good enough. The departure of the match-winning Robbie Keane before the start of the season and the failure to adequately replace Gary McAllister's influence, both on and off the field, had been decisive. Keane was sold to Internazionale for an enormous £13 million. Noel Whelan also joined Middlesbrough. It was asking a lot of Craig Bellamy, who had only recently recovered from serious injury, to step up a division to such instant effect as Keane. The call for John Hartson in February was more than just a scrawny cry, City had long been interested in the player. However, the state of his legs had turned him into an insurance nightmare and the transfer stretched Bryan Richardson's ingenuity to the limit. He was eventually acquired on a deal that gave Wimbledon £15,000 a match, up to a maximum of £5 million, for every game played. Had City been able to call on Hartson earlier, things might have been different.

Earnest attempts had been made to bolster the squad at the outset but projected deals obstinately fell through. Those involving Jorg Albertz and Neil McCann of Glasgow Rangers led to recrimination between the two clubs. David Thompson was signed from Liverpool but the team struggled from the start. It was always a battle too many.

In the wake of relegation, the squad was reshaped. Bellamy, after a disappointing season, was sold to Newcastle at a profit on the £6 million paid to Norwich for him. He was replaced by Lee Hughes, West Brom having to accept a fee of £5,000,001. Julian Joachim arrived from Villa as the make weight in exchange for Hadji and promtly joined the ranks of players badly injured in ill-conceived pre-season friendlies. Opening day victory at Stockport was followed with home defeat by Wolves. Poor results put pressure on Gordon Strachan. Some felt that the chairman had been loyal for too long.

Strachan lost his job just before September 11. In his strengths as a player lay perhaps his undoing as a manager – an unwillingness to delegate, to stand back, to let go. Surprisingly, his team appeared to lack fitness and, as was demonstrated at Villa Park, the ability to step up a gear when required. He later conceded that he had placed too much emphasis on mental preparation at Coventry, not enough on the physical. It had reached a point where you could be certain that City would not win if the opposition scored first. Indeed, there was not a single instance during Strachan's last 9 League games in charge of the Sky Blues overturning their opponents' lead.

Strachan did not readily make peace with those with whom he fell out. The ill-fated signing of Colin Hendry occurred at a time when Gary Breen had invited disfavour. Strachan was also accused of playing people out of position and of tactical inflexibility.

'I wish I had known the time to go at Coventry. All managers have a sell-by date but at Coventry, it could be argued that I allowed mine to be delayed too long. For the good of my own career and the prospects of the team, I possibly should have left in the summer of 2000', wrote Strachan. Never let it be forgotten though that through the windmill of those touchline gesticulations his teams provided us with some very special moments.

A few months later, amid the growing threat of administration, Bryan Richardson was deposed as chairman. Richardson had worked strenuously to enhance the club's profile in an attempt to enable Coventry City, if not to become one of the big players in English football, then at least to reach a position where it could expect to consign regular last-day nightmares to the past.

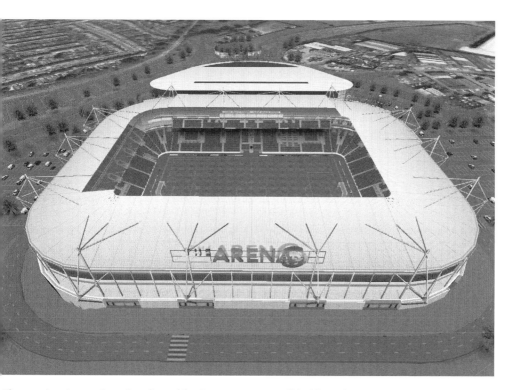

The vast American-style casino planned for Coventry's Arena will be like nothing Britain has ever seen before. People are expected to travel for miles to play on its gaming tables and many slot machines.'

His vision courted risk and assumed three things: being able to build a new stadium and get it open on time, avoiding relegation, and the commercial value of the game being sustained. Ambitious plans for a retractable pitch and roof were shelved but the stadium was still delayed by several years. The team was relegated, and the economic contraction of football – illustrated by the collapse of ITVDigital – threatened the very existence of many clubs. Coventry, who like others had borrowed and invested heavily in transfer fees and salaries to ensure their prized status in the Premier League, faced a massive debt.

As fans, we deem it a privilege worthy of the gods to be running our favourite club. At Coventry City, the board paid their chief executive a good salary. Although it did not put Bryan Richardson on even the substitutes' bench of top wage-earners at the club, there was a growing feeling among supporters that such a salary – alongside other benefits – amounted to a blasphemy.

Few clubs or fans had yet begun to grasp the literal implication of survival that afternoon at Villa Park. How the landscape has changed.

ROCHDALE v. COVENTRY CITY

25 January 2003
Spotland
FA Cup Fourth Round
Rochdale 2 Coventry City 0

This was the demoralising turning-point of a puzzling and very distressing season. Twice before, Rochdale had played Calvary to Coventry. The big cemetery in Gracie Fields' home town is overlooked by the Cemetery Hotel. After this humiliating defeat, it was difficult to believe that Coventry could ever rise again.

In 1971, Coventry commemorated the fiftieth anniversary of their first FA Cup defeat at Rochdale with a repeat performance. Noel Cantwell reacted to the draw by asking 'Where's Rochdale?' He then refused to play under the Spotland floodlights. The game was eventually played early on a Monday afternoon with 13,011 people turning out to see the home side win 2-1. When City lost 1-0 at Rochdale in the League Cup in 1991, they had at least made sure of winning the first leg 4-0. Rochdale even won the only League game played at Spotland between the two clubs in 1926.

Two late Cardiff goals at Ninian Park had forced a replay in the third round. At Highfield Road, the quality of City's three goals and the ability to take the chances at such crucial moments led many to believe that the Sky Blues were on course for a good Cup run and also a play-off position.

City were desperately lucky to take a last-ditch point at Nottingham Forest the week before Rochdale. But if the side could play so badly and still conjure a point through a beautifully contrived goal by Juan Sara, we were right to be optimistic. The Argentinian Sara, one of City's stream of loan players, lifted his top to reveal a 'Jesus loves you' T-shirt. Sara, theologically a sort of latter-day George Boateng, had set a trend with such shirts in the club shop at Dundee.

Rochdale, with an eleven who were making up the numbers in the Third Division, were simply more up for it than the Sky Blues. They were soon taking the game to the visitors with a number of goal attempts. Richie Partridge, one of City's most successful loan signings, swapped wings in an attempt to make more of an impression but, just after the half-hour, Rochdale took a deserved lead. Mo Konjic dribbled characteristically into his opponents' half but was dispossessed by Gareth Griffiths. David Flitcroft's long ball sprung Paul Connor on the counter attack. Connor retained his composure and fired an angled shot past Morten Hyldgaard in the City goal. Further chances came and went on both sides but Rochdale's half-time lead was creating more than a mumble. Within moments of the restart it turned to a rumble when City went 2 down. Player/manager Paul Simpson hit a corner to the far post where centre half Griffiths timed his run perfectly to head past Hyldgaard. Connor and the giant Clive Platt continued to threaten the City defence. The 3,300 travelling supporters grew silent as the home side continued to carve out chances. City made three separate substitutions but the passing was poor and the strikers as blunt as broken matches. The story was set for the rest of the season.

Nobody could possibly imagine that the team would emulate the collapse of the previous year let alone to what extent. Coventry had already started their worst sequence of results since that terrible initial season in the Football League in 1919/20. After teatime on Boxing Day, City only managed one further League win in their remaining 21 League games – it came at bottom-of-the-table Grimsby, courtesy of an own-goal and a penalty. In 13 of those games, City failed to score. Only 11 more points and 12 more goals were scored. The Sky Blues would have finished several points adrift at the bottom of the table if the season had started during the indigestion of Christmas.

Above left: Gary McAllister.

Above right: Mo Konjic.

Only one team scored fewer goals during the season. Eleven home games were lost and not one of the last ten was won. Such statistics speak for themselves. Injuries to influential players such as Youssef Safri and Craig Hignett were significant, but only a detail in the wider picture. The club got through forty-four players during the season, one more even than in 1919/20. This was due in part to the number of loan players and the blooding of youngsters.

Gary McAllister took over as manager from Roland Nilsson at the end of the previous season under no illusions about the constraints. There was a lot of knee-jerk talk about his lack of experience, as if a couple of years in the sticks could be the mystical means to wisdom and judgement. Sadly, for family reasons, he resigned in January 2004. He was succeeded by his assistant, Eric Black, who was in time to preside over another disaster in the Cup, at Colchester. Black, in turn, was controversially dismissed before the end of the season and replaced by Peter Reid.

One topic overshadowed all others during the course of the 2002/03 season, affecting the team directly or indirectly, and that was the financial survival of the club. Coventry were drawing in their belts after their trousers had dropped. It could have been worse, much worse. Had the collapse of the transfer market occurred a year earlier, it is possible that the club might have gone under. It was the sales that were made after relegation that were vital. Chris Kirkland went to Liverpool in a deal that could eventually realise £9 million. Once promotion again became an impossibility, the club were faced with the need to excise all of those on Premiership wages. It had become necessary to throw the pieces up in the air and start again from scratch.

The departure of Gordon Strachan and the unseating of Bryan Richardson dominated the 2001/02 season. Richardson could be seen on the huge television screen at Selhurst Park punching the air as Hall, Bothroyd and McSheffrey scored memorable goals. The following day, the rug was pulled from under him.

Richardson reluctantly saw off Strachan whom he replaced with the mild-mannered Roland Nilsson. Jim Smith was eventually appointed as Nilsson's No.2 but the team looked spineless. The challenges facing the new chairman could not have been greater but Mike McGinnity addressed the desperate financial situation with tenacity and increasing effect.

Mike McGinnity.

Eric Black.

Roland Nilsson.

Peter Reid.

Afterword

Football of 120 years ago survives only in sepia and print, but a museum of memory and humanity is sustained through its bequest. Whatever we divine through the parabola of a ball was transcended for Coventry City and its followers by the events of 1987 and by a position amongst the elite of English football spread over five decades. It was under Harry Storer and, more than anyone, Jimmy Hill, that the club reached out for those fields. It fell to Cantwell, Milne, Sillett, Strachan and others to cultivate them.

Meanwhile, the football business has changed out of all recognition. Clubs make increasing demands on the loyalty and pockets of their supporters. Contrary to popular perception, there is not much difference in price between a seat at a Premier League match and most seats at the opera. And how many people go to nineteen operas a year? The need to nurture its identity and image is football's abiding challenge in a world, the real world, where riches jostle with ruin.

May is the cruellest month. For so many years, springtime survival represented success for the Sky Blues, hanging on to that treasured and deserved status the end in itself. One day, the end really came. When it did, the experience affected everyone connected with the football club. Gordon Strachan once observed how you could 'smell' relegation on people. Coventry City is only now beginning to disinfect itself.

The sky was the limit in 1967, and 1987 a reaffirmation. When will reality again play handmaiden to our dreams?

Harry Barratt and Alf Wood.

Coventry City Greats

GEORGE ROWLANDS

Over six thousand players have proudly worn the colours of Coventry City since the club was first formed as Singer's FC back in 1883. This volume offers a retrospective look at 100 of the finest players to have represented the club, with a detailed examination of their time at Coventry and their careers in football.

978 0 7524 2294 4

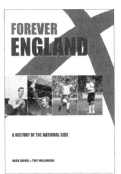

Forever England

MARK SHAOUL & TONY WILLIAMSON

The definitive history of the English national side. From the days of the amateur gentlemen of the 1870s to the present day, Forever England is an insightful and fascinating account of the history of the country's national football team, covers the careers of England's all-time greats and is an essential read for everyone who is interested in the history of the Three Lions.

978 0 7524 2939 6

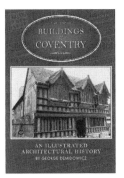

Buildings of Coventry

GEORGE DEMIDOWICZ

The buildings featured within cover almost a millennium of Coventry's history. There are one thousand statutory and locally listed buildings in the city and many of these are splendid examples of their period. This book describes and illustrates some of the finest examples that can be seen today and will serve as a useful guide for those wishing to explore and learn more about the city's history through its buildings.

978 0 7524 3155 3

Warwickshire CCC Greats

ROBERT BROOKE

Since Warwickshire's first and only bona fide cricket club was formed at Lamington Spa's Regent Hotel on 8 April 1882, it has enjoyed a chequered record of success and failure. There can, however, be no argument about the individual ability of the players who have represented the club over the decades. This volume looks back and recognises the achievements of the men whose contributions made the county.

978 7524 2180 8